Disrupt
This
!

Karen J. Head

Disrupt This

!

MOOCS AND THE PROMISES

OF TECHNOLOGY

University Press of New England | Hanover and London

University Press of New England
www.upne.com
© 2017 University Press of New England
All rights reserved
Manufactured in the United States of America
Designed by Mindy Basinger Hill
Typeset in Garamond Premier Pro

For permission to reproduce any of the material in this book,
contact Permissions, University Press of New England,
One Court Street, Suite 250, Lebanon NH 03766;
or visit www.upne.com.

Library of Congress Cataloging-in-Publication Data
available upon request

5   4   3   2   1

This book is dedicated to all college instructors,

past, present, and future

(especially the ones who taught me),

and to our students.

This book is also in memory of Bob Bergstrom,

who told me to never stop believing in *someday*

and encouraged me to fly.

Contents

Acknowledgments

Writing a book takes up a considerable amount of professional and personal time, and the people in a writer's life take part in the process even though it isn't their project. Throughout this book, I use a series of movie references, and just like actors who win film awards and continue talking even when the exit music begins playing, I am sure I will forget to thank some of the many people who have helped me as I have written this book, so please forgive any omission. I have received so much good advice, and I have benefitted from support from a variety of people and organizations. Some of you contributed ideas, some of you read drafts, some of you provided resources, and some of you just listened. I am grateful to every one of you.

Thanks to my editor, Richard Pult, production editor, Susan Abel, and copyeditor, Joyce Parks, as well as many other people at University Press of New England for believing in my project and working with me to make my draft into a much better book.

Without the generous support provided by the Bill & Melinda Gates Foundation and the Georgia Institute of Technology's Office of the Provost for the *First-Year Composition 2.0* MOOC, this book would not exist. I also appreciate the support I received from the technology staff at Worcester College, Oxford, who helped arrange for me to teach the final two weeks of the MOOC while I was in England. This book also would not exist if not for my co-principal investigators, Rebecca Burnett and Andy Frazee, our amazing MOOC team, and our technology coordinator, Pam Buffington. All of you gave so much of yourselves during our MOOC adventure.

Research support for this book was provided by the Ivan Allen College of Liberal Arts and the School of Literature, Communication, and Culture at the Georgia Institute of Technology. Thanks to my dean, Jacqueline Royster, and my chair, Richard Utz, for providing me the tools for success, and to Sam Aral for finding me that secret little space where I could work undisturbed.

Portions of this book were completed during two residencies at the Hambidge Center for the Creative Arts and Sciences. I am grateful to have been selected as a fellow.

Thanks to Carolyn Mooney at the *Chronicle of Higher Education* for providing me the opportunity to publish my series of blog posts and articles on teaching a MOOC that were the seed work for this book.

Throughout the last four years, the team in the Georgia Tech Office of Institute Communications, especially Jason Maderer and Michael Warden, have been incredibly kind in their "handling" of me and my work. Thanks for being such wonderful colleagues.

After our MOOC ended, the research for this book took nearly two years. No one helped more with that process than Justin Dehorty, my intrepid undergraduate research assistant, who exceeded my expectations in every way. I will never forget the day he wrote a small computer program to get me the information I needed. Wow!

Without question, the group of people who deserve the most thanks are the professional staff who have worked in the Communication Center over the past five years. Without your willingness to support me and protect my time, this book would never have been completed. Brandy, Peter, Clint, Joy, Chris, Julie, Leah, Becky, Noah, Dustin, Sarah, Caitlin, Joshua, James, Ruthie, Jennifer, Malavika, LeeAnn, Aron, Nirmal, Lauren, Michael, Carlos, Jane, and Melissa, I am indebted to each of you more than I can ever say. Every single one of you is amazing!

On a more personal note, I want to thank my health care team, Dr. Jefrey Lieberman, Dr. Walton Reeves, Dr. Harry Delcher, Dr. Larry Phillips, Dr. Sharon Mathis, Hope, Justus, and the many other doctors, nurses, and specialists who helped me manage chronic illness through a stressful time. Thanks also to the most caring (and fashionable) veterinary team in the world, Ormewood Animal Hospital, for helping care for two elderly cats.

I am also very fortunate to have so many smart and funny friends who have been there for me throughout this project: Collin, JC, Bob, Blake, Carol S., Nihad, Lisa, Janet, Carol C., Jay T., Paul, Jenny, Brian, Jay B., Cari, Rusty, Shawn, Kristi, Scott, Marilyn, Danny, Janine, Nina, Janis, Randi, Thomas,

Walter, Julia, Sibylle, Iris-Aya, Martina, Yves, Steven, Felipe, Carol M., Linda, Bill P., Grace, Philip, Ellen, Beki, Keith, Annie, Liz, Anne-Françoise, Jeff, Bill T., Cheryl, Dan, Tucker, Agnes, Lorelei, Paris, and Jade.

Everything about my present is a testament to my past, and I am grateful to have a family who cheers for me no matter what: Mom, Dad, Mike, Maureen, Jason, Steef, Helen, Rose, Henry, Dot, Dick, Mark, Harry, and Emma. I love you all.

Finally, I want to thank my husband, Colin—there simply aren't words enough of gratitude or love. Thank you for always asking the right questions, and for reminding me I was never alone when looking for the answers, especially the difficult ones.

Disrupt
This
!

How Did a Nice Girl Like You
Wind Up Here?

In the fall of 2012, I received a Georgia Institute of Technology email invitation to a town hall meeting about our new Massive Open Online Course (MOOC) initiative. I remember being annoyed about the meeting, not because of the topic per se, but because it necessitated the rescheduling of a meeting with a student who needed my help on an assignment. Nevertheless, I felt I should go—partly because an inner voice told me, "I know you don't think this has anything to do with you, but it actually does."

The meeting was held in the large lecture room located in the Klaus Building, one of the facilities belonging to our College of Computing. The location seemed appropriate given the technology topic, but the room was not large enough for the entire faculty, much less the entire university community, so for an institute-wide town hall, it was an odd choice. It was a packed house—standing room only. When I glanced around the room, I noticed a few interesting things. There were many administrators (vice-provosts, deans, school chairs, and directors) in attendance, but not our president. I recognized many academic professionals (what we call our full-time, non-tenure-track faculty). Several members of the faculty from the College of Computing were there—not surprising given that the first two faculty members to offer a MOOC at Georgia Tech were from that college. Otherwise, the faculty showing was noticeably sparse. There was a smattering of students, most of whom looked older and were probably graduate students. Several of the Brittain Postdoctoral Teaching Fellows from the School of Literature, Media, and Communication (my home unit), many who (I knew) engaged in digital humanities scholarship, were grouped together like a phalanx blocking one of the back doors. As we waited for the meeting to begin, I was busy with my iPhone, emailing my student a clarification about her upcoming assignment.

Our provost, Rafael Bras, took the microphone and welcomed us. He made a few remarks about the exciting opportunity being presented to the institute. Once again, Georgia Tech would be on the front end of an exciting technological advancement; in this case we were going to help reframe the idea of higher education, something we were particularly prepared to do, given our history as a leading technological university, he explained. Then he turned over the meeting to Richard DeMillo, who had been named director of the Center for 21st Century Universities (C21U), which was created in 2011.

What followed was not so much a town hall meeting as a public relations presentation. DeMillo talked about his own past in the corporate world, and asked how many of us remembered the Netscape browser. He explained that it had been a good product, but ultimately it wasn't able to compete; that was okay because better products were developed in its wake, he said. The implication was that a university education could be compared to a software application, and that we should look to the tech industry for advice and inspiration. As a rhetorician, I found myself paying closer attention because this meeting was beginning to feel highly scripted.

DeMillo then called a small group to the stage. Seated on high, stool-like chairs were two faculty members from Interactive Computing, Tucker Balch and Irfan Essa. Joining them was an instructional designer from our Office of Distance Education, Fatima Wirth. (When a colleague leaned over and asked, "We have a distance ed program?" I suppressed a smile, and reflected that to many of our faculty, distance education is tangential and inconsequential to the mission of the academy.) Their MOOCs were to be the first ones offered from Georgia Tech: Balch would teach a computational finance class; Essa would teach a course on computational photography; and Wirth would teach a course on how to teach MOOCs. (Wirth's ill-fated course turned into a self-inflicted black eye when problems with the online chat rooms required Georgia Tech to suspend it within days of its launch. It has never restarted.) The panelists briefly introduced themselves and offered a few details about their courses. At this point, I realized this wasn't so much a meeting to discuss the possible future of MOOCs at Georgia Tech, but rather an information session about how we were already committed to providing them. The Q&A session was short and mostly polite. Only a couple of faculty members expressed anything akin to pushback. I returned to my office thinking my intuition had been wrong, and that MOOCs had nothing to do with me.

A few hours later, everything about my professional life would change. I was sitting on a bench in one of the campus courtyards admiring a large ginkgo already beginning to drop its leaves. I was waiting for the director of our Writing and Communication Program, Rebecca Burnett. She had caught me right after the MOOC town hall and asked to meet me in the afternoon. We frequently met, so I didn't think much about it. She arrived and after a brief exchange of pleasantries, she said, "There is a request for proposals from the Gates Foundation to teach MOOCs focused on general education. We are going to submit a proposal for teaching first-year writing. I've spoken to Richard [our school chair], and we think you should be the instructor." I remember having a jumble of thoughts, most of which centered around the idea that my brand-new school chair and my most closely connected disciplinary, and senior, colleague had decided that I should do this ridiculously new thing. I was teaching an extra course already that fall to help cover for a faculty member on leave in the department. Consequently, I was to have the spring semester free from teaching. This was good thing because I needed to focus on research toward tenure. "I'm supposed to be doing research this spring, so I don't think I'm the right person for this," I said. "Rebecca, you should do it." She put her hand on my arm and smiled. "No, it must be you. You are the perfect choice. You'll be great on camera. And this *is* research. I'll be there for the whole project, helping every step of the way." I recollect saying no several more times. She told me to go home and think it over. She'd need my final answer the following day. I left campus that afternoon convinced that accepting this assignment was the worst possible thing I could do. It was going to be a huge commitment, and I wasn't sure that many of my colleagues would think this was a good use of my time, either. No matter how interesting an adventure in teaching (the thing I love most about my job) this might be, I kept reminding myself that teaching is not the primary focus for tenure decisions at a research university. I simply had to be firm and decline.

That evening over dinner, I recounted the events of the day to my husband, who happens to be a tenured faculty member in our College of Computing and an institute-wide administrator. I assumed he would agree with me wholeheartedly. Instead, he asked me the question that would change my mind: "Are you prepared to let others tell you whether teaching on a platform like this works—especially if they are already convinced it *will* work?" I realized in that moment that if I ever wanted to be part of the conversation, a conversation that had clearly already begun, and if I wanted people to take what I had to say seriously, then I had to be part of the process. "Sleep on it," he said.

The experiences I will detail throughout this book are the result of my decision to engage in this process, rather than stand on the sidelines.

ONE

The Rhetoric of Punditry

There's a tsunami coming.

JOHN L. HENNESSY | President, Stanford University

When the president of one of the most elite universities in the world, a president who also sits on the boards of companies like Google, gives an interview in the *New Yorker* and declares that he will be spending his sabbatical considering how online education may disrupt the ways that universities distinguish themselves, even universities like Stanford, people take notice.

With a growing emphasis on the notion of *disrupting* higher education, it is no surprise that alarmist metaphors like "impending tsunamis" quickly became common. Almost certainly Hennessy would have known about the theory of *disruptive innovation* detailed by Clayton Christensen in his 1997 book, *The Innovator's Dilemma: When New Technologies Cause Great Firms to Fail.*[1] Christensen defines the concept by saying, "*Disruptive innovation* describes a process by which a product or service takes root initially in simple applications at the bottom of a market and then relentlessly moves up market, eventually displacing established competitors."[2] In that spirit, innovators began to consider how technology might disrupt higher education, and new online models for providing educational content became a cause célèbre.

Drawing the most attention were platforms called Massive Open Online Courses, or MOOCs. In May of 2012, Thomas Friedman wrote an article about MOOCs titled "Come the Revolution," describing the Coursera startup at Stanford and explaining how that platform and others like it (EdX and Udacity) were about to completely change higher education. He declared, "In five years this will be a huge industry," and, "Let the revolution begin."[3] Only six months later, Laura Pappano would label 2012 the Year of the MOOC.[4] Another two months would pass, and Friedman would weigh in with yet another MOOC-focused article, "Revolution Hits the Universities," proclaiming:

Nothing has more potential to lift more people out of poverty—by providing them an affordable education to get a job or improve in the job they have. Nothing has more potential to unlock a billion more brains to solve the world's biggest problems. And nothing has more potential to enable us to reimagine higher education than the massive open online course, or MOOC, platforms that are being developed by the likes of Stanford and the Massachusetts Institute of Technology and companies like Coursera and Udacity.[5]

Readers could hardly ignore such lofty promises for the future of higher education. Friedman ends this article with a quote from Massachusetts Institute of Technology president Rafael Reif: "There is a new world unfolding, and everyone will have to adapt." In only one year, the touting of MOOCs had grown swiftly. Oddly, the imagery was almost always associated with destruction—discussions were replete with language about revolution, disruption, and even natural disaster—a tsunami indeed.

My university, the Georgia Institute of Technology, was one of the first to join a cadre of elite schools on the Coursera platform. It was a source of great administrative pride at Georgia Tech that its online master's degree in computer science, which is hosted on Udacity's platform, was the front-page feature of an issue of the *New York Times*.[6] Similarly, other universities have aligned themselves with platforms like EdX and NovoEd.

Indeed, university administrators' eagerness to align their institutions with MOOCs and similar technologies remains a fashion that schools ignore at their peril. One need only look to Theresa Sullivan's firing and rehiring at the University of Virginia as evidence of the rush to judgment and the need to be "on the train" no matter where it's going.[7] For now, it seems enough for some universities to say they are on the bandwagon—that they have a place within a new technological utopia.

No matter how inflated the claims and how unfocused the business decisions may have been during the first three years of MOOC mania, there are genuine concerns driving the development of these technological experiments. As tuition costs increase and state university boards demand grand educational technology schemes that demonstrate a commitment to open access, more universities find themselves needing to provide more for less (at least in appearance). Most people understand that lowering costs is a goal of university boards, especially those which must answer to state legislative bodies. But more of what? More lectures? More lab time? More conferences with faculty? More academic support? More opportunities to engage with other students? More extracurricular programs and facilities? The college experience transcends what happens in the classroom in many ways. Everyone involved in the conversations about improving higher education will first need to agree on what our common goals, explicitly defined, will be.

The next development in these platforms is likely to be nontechnological: the policy battle over whether and under what circumstances MOOCs and MOOC-like courses can be taken for university credit. In 2015, the Texas State University System introduced a new "free first year" plan: nontraditional students are encouraged to take MOOCs in order to complete their first year of college. The only costs for the students, reportedly $90 per class, are for the Advanced Placement Exam or College-Level Placement Exam that each student must pass in order to receive course credit. According to a report in the *Texas Tribune,* the Texas State University System chancellor, Brian Mc-Call, is not concerned about some of the often-expressed criticisms about dropout rates and cheating:

> McCall said he isn't worried. Since courses are free, the cost of failing to fin-
> ish one is much smaller than it would be for students dropping a class. And
> someone who cheated in an online class would still have to pass the highly
> moderated AP or CLEP test, he said. The Texas State System hasn't set many
> expectations for the program. McCall said he has no idea how many will
> sign up or actually receive credit. But he said he's thrilled to give students the
> opportunity. "We believe this will require more discipline, more focus, more
> resolve to get the desired result."[8]

Carefully monitoring programs like the one in Texas will be important for establishing whether students are finding new pathways to success, or if this is just another way for a university system to "be on board" with programs that are appealing to legislators and pundits.

From Disruption to Reform

Many of the discussions about MOOCs tend to take a "for" or "against" stance: FOR: Scale, Democratization, Technology Imperatives; AGAINST: Impersonal Approach, Unsuitability for Humanities. Such dichotomous reasoning is fueled by appeals to the concept of *disruptive innovation*. Disruption is so clear and sudden when compared with reform that it is no surprise that pundits arguing for disruptive change in higher education have been happy to polarize discussions and to portray caution as opposition or any skepticism about technological determinism as Luddite foot-dragging. My goal in this book is to inject some proportionality into the claims in favor of MOOCs.

I speak from experience.

In November 2012, I was part of a team that was awarded a grant by the Bill & Melinda Gates Foundation to develop a MOOC for one of the most ubiquitous of university courses: first-year writing, or what is often called freshman composition. It was a deliberate challenge: Could we transform the high-touch culture of the composition classroom into a massively scaled experience online? Could we learn more about teaching tuition-paying and grades-conscious university students from the experience of teaching thousands of casual, online walk-ins? Could we satisfactorily teach students how to communicate more effectively by using an educational platform that had been designed with science, technology, engineering, and mathematics (STEM) subject matter in mind (or, at least, subject matter with easily articulated right and wrong answers)? Over the following several months, while designing and teaching the MOOC, I also wrote about our process in a series of articles published by the *Chronicle of Higher Education*. I chose this practice of both doing and reflecting in action[9] as a rhetorical engagement in and with MOOCs because, by contrast with punditry, it is more likely to lead to a fair appreciation of the opportunities and obstacles that this highly commoditized and granular approach to higher education presents.

Experience is a great generator of nuance. Rather than focus on whether to dismantle current educational structures or leave things as they are, I want to see us shift to arguments about strengthening our practices—that is, we should first use technology to enhance what already works well in classrooms, rather than resort to an approach that "throws away the baby with the bath-water," which would only create a new set of problems.

Not Invented Here

The idea of offering open access and free educational services isn't a new one for those of us who work in writing centers. (The Communication Center at Georgia Tech, which I direct, is my fifth experience in a university writing or tutoring center.) My writing center colleagues have been working within open access for decades, for both internal and external constituencies. However, our services have often been marginalized, relegated to the far corners and dank basements of campuses, where staff had to learn to make do. Online Writing Labs (OWLS), like the long-established one at Purdue,[10] have been offering free tutorial advice and resources to the public since the dawn of the Internet. OWLS may not seem particularly "cutting-edge" now, but such platforms are among the progenitors of MOOCs. More recently, a newer-model OWL from Excelsior College[11] has managed to leverage its institution's vast distance learning programs to create an interactive OWL that includes special iPad apps and gaming technology. Essentially, OWLS began as a static collection of helpful hyperlinks, but have evolved into downloadable materials and interactive instructional modules.

In fact, writing centers have much to teach those who champion MOOCs. While writing center directors and tutors have long supported the idea of open source material sharing, they also know that the critical work they do is in the day-to-day, one-on-one tutoring they provide—a model that is the antithesis of large-scale student support. One-on-one tutoring provides one of the most personalized forms of learning support, in that every pedagogical move is focused on the exact needs of a particular student. Providing resources in a free and open environment is a good thing, but doing so without recognizing the need to help students appropriately choose and negotiate the available information is less advisable. What any writing center director could have told any MOOC course developer is that you must have a carefully constructed balance between merely delivering content and catering to each student's particular pedagogical needs and preferred mode of personal interaction.

Likewise, professionals in established and successful distance learning programs should be part of the conversation about any proposed innovations in higher education delivery methods. Much more attention and *voice* need to be given to distance learning experts like Thomas Reeves from the School of Education at the University of Georgia, or Curtis Bonk from the School of Education at Indiana University, whose scholarship on the subject is extensive. It is astounding that distance learning pioneers have been largely ignored in the pressure to portray MOOCs as new, and it is ironic that most of the people teaching MOOCs have had little or no experience in teaching online in nonmassive, pre-MOOC contexts.[12] I was no exception in this regard.

After attending conferences and reading work by distance learning professionals and scholars since I taught my MOOC, I have learned one critical thing: it would have been better to consult with them *before* I ever attempted to design and deliver a MOOC. In fact, it was naive of us to move forward without consulting the long-established experts. I am to blame for not asking this question about our team. Perhaps the implosion of the MOOC about the fundamentals of online education at Georgia Tech (in which the instructor attempted to have students use a form in Google Docs, which could not handle such large numbers)[13] made me think that distance education professionals were also making things up as they went along, but I should have considered that we, like other elite schools, might be the least likely to have a distance learning team that was at the forefront of technology and innovation in online learning. After all, the teaching practices of research universities are aimed at the economically advantaged and academically accomplished residential students who make up the vast majority of their populations, not the nontraditional students who most need distance education. Perhaps the bubble in which many of us who are fortunate enough to teach at an elite school reside lulls us into the sense that we can do anything. In retrospect, more humility was called for.

So why aren't more people acknowledging the role that distance learning professionals, as well as writing centers and their staff members, have been playing for years? Generally speaking, no one pays much attention to service-based academic programs. I hesitate to speak for distance learning professionals, but in my limited experience, I suspect the problem is that in many schools the primary focus remains on the students on campus, although this is changing as flipped and hybrid classrooms for all students become more popular (albeit sometimes more popular with administrators than with faculty or students). In the case of writing centers, many faculty members and administrators have seen them as places designed solely to provide remediation—places to help underperforming and struggling students "get by" as best they can. Consequently, the funding and other support for such centers often have been quite low. Writing center directors are accustomed to providing much for little. Also, I would argue that because the focus of writing centers is on communication (even across disciplines), they offer a service that is less "fashionable" than tutorials on topics like Coursera's "Bitcoin and Cryptocurrency Technologies," or EdX's "Quality of Life: Livability in Future Cities," or Udacity's "App Monetization."

But excellent communication is the foundation for any successful online course. Whatever the topic—writing an essay, crafting a business pitch, or mastering client-server architectures—none is going to resonate unless those who prepare these new instructional materials do so with a keen sense of the rhetoric behind what they are doing. Without considering the elements of multimodality and multiliteracies, courses or tutorials are nothing more than a glamorized version of a stale lecture with some bullet-pointed slides. A 2014 study[14] confirmed that such lectures are not effective. One response to the study sums up the views of many instructors, from traditional and online environments: " 'This is a really important article—the impression I get is that it's almost unethical to be lecturing if you have this data,' says Eric Mazur, a physicist at Harvard University who has campaigned against stale lecturing techniques for 27 years and was not involved in the work. 'It's good to see such a cohesive picture emerge from their meta-analysis—an abundance of proof that lecturing is outmoded, outdated, and inefficient.' "[15] If instructors (and designers) do not reflect on their practices more carefully, their online courses, no matter how seemingly innovative, will be as "outmoded, outdated, and inefficient" as the traditional classroom courses they are meant to replace.

Designers often become enamored with innovations and neglect the more mundane needs of their clients. A fashionable friend of mine once purchased a space-age-looking sofa covered in a striking shade of chartreuse. Three months later she accepted that the design was uncomfortable and the dramatic color was fading in spots. No number of throw pillows could make it okay. She had difficulty giving the sofa away; even charity shops didn't want it. Finally, an artist friend took it, stripped it down, and used the parts for a project. Her experience put me in mind of my decision to buy a kneeling seat to replace my office chair in the early 1990s. As more people found themselves hunched at computers all day, kneelers were marketed as the next generation of office seating—just as the term *ergonomic* became popular. I used my kneeler for a couple of months before putting it in a storage closet. Innovation is exciting for designers, but ultimately, I just wanted a comfortable place to sit. And so it is with learners and educational technologists. MOOCs introduce glitzy technology into the "delivery" of education, but in the process may sacrifice its very purpose.

Punditry

My goal is to analyze the rhetoric of those who talk about online courses, myself included, and I will inject myself into this discourse in the first person, entering into an extended dialogue with several commentators, especially the writers of two influential books published in 2011: *The Innovative University: Changing the DNA of Higher Education from the Inside Out,* by Clayton Christensen and Henry Eyring,[16] and *Abelard to Apple: The Fate of American Colleges and Universities,* by Richard DeMillo.[17] My choice of these particular texts is a result of having had them recommended to me when MOOC mania unexpectedly became a part of my life. These were the two most widely read books that I read at the beginning. I use them here as illustrations of a wider conversation—that is, they represent a *type* of common discourse seen throughout the disruption genre. I also chose these particular source materials because the authors have continued to speak about the issues at hand; they continue to be part of the national conversation about disruption in higher education. My eyewitness testimony will serve as a counterpoint to their often perceptive and contextually informed punditry, but punditry nonetheless—removed from the day-to-day experience of actually teaching many thousands of students, nearly twenty-two thousand in the MOOC that I taught. When one has been in the field or gone through a significant and novel experience, it is natural to resent armchair Fraziers writing their

Golden Boughs from the comfort of their studies. Stepping back and generalizing from experience is essential, but experience is where you have to start.

It is important to investigate how discussions, such as those about higher education, get started and gain steam. Of course, all authors and all members of the higher education community have agendas. One would hope so: that is a matter of being engaged in any conversation worth investing one's career in. However, the role pundits play is different and starker. Whether accidentally or deliberately, their adoption of strong positions renders their ideas quotable and easily digested. Nothing helps more if you want to become a rock star in your field than making exaggerated and simplified claims to provoke your audience. Having something to sell—a MOOC platform, or your speaking engagements—almost requires this.

Getting Us on Their Side

An important rhetorical move as a writer, known since the Sophists of ancient Greece, is to establish your ethos. You want your audience to consider you credible. Bold claims stated without qualifications or evidence can make you sound authoritative, as long as you do not draw attention to the thinness of the ice on which you are skating. But it is important not to browbeat your audience into acquiescence. You achieve your aim by becoming "likable" in whatever ways you think your intended audience will respond to. Some politicians (even some authors) may be deliberately Machiavellian in their deployment of ethos-promoting devices, but this need not be so. Simply adopting a relaxed, amiable voice does wonders for one's aura of authenticity, and therefore (although the one does not necessarily follow from the other) authoritativeness.

This method is used throughout *The Innovative University*. Christensen and Eyring walk a careful line between portraying themselves as erudite authorities in the field of higher education and being "regular guys" interested in all the day-to-day concerns that an average parent, teacher, or student might have. By the end of my first reading I found myself liking the writers, whom I've never met. While I disagree with much of what they say, and I will touch on many of these disagreements later, I am positively disposed toward their apparently genuine enthusiasm and sincere desire to help improve higher education.

Another approach to enhancing ethos is to tire your audience into skimming only the takeaway points. Authors do this by writing at length and offering a running digest of their points using highlighting devices, such as chapter summaries, suggestive section headings, and graphically distinct callouts. Christensen and Eyring are guilty of this. *The Innovative University* is a long book, 401 pages plus notes. Essentially it is divided into two halves. The first is about the histories of Harvard and BYU-Idaho (formerly Ricks College), which are presented as case studies for the ways higher education has evolved in the United States. This half seeks to inform people outside the academy how and why universities have come to function in the ways they do. One could even describe this half of the book as nostalgic—yet another story of how America became a great nation, in this case by way of building its higher education system.

The second half of the book details the need for and suggests models for disruptive innovation, a theory advanced by Christensen. It targets an audience of people inside the academy. The shift in content, language, and tone is directed toward people who are likely to be threatened by the proposed changes.

Few people are likely to read such a long book in its entirety. Policy makers and senior administrators, accustomed to easily digested white papers or executive summaries, are unlikely to complete it. Instead they will skim the callout boxes, charts, graphs, tables, and summaries. And yet without the complete context, Christensen and Eyring's ideas might sound far better than they are. One example of this will suffice for now. As I explore in Chapter 9, the BYU-Idaho model is not sustainable without the guarantee of an abundance of volunteers. The Church of Jesus Christ of Latter-day Saints' (the Mormon Church's) expectation of volunteerism played a critical role in the transformation of BYU-Idaho. A close reading of the text makes this fact abundantly clear, but the authors do not draw attention to it, perhaps because, as members of the church themselves, they take it for granted.

Yet another standard rhetorical technique—this one coming under the rubric of pathos—is to address the audience's supposed concerns by giving them information or advice that is of special value to them. Naturally, this requires a writer to gauge an audience carefully. By the final chapters, *The Innovative University* sounds less like a critique of the higher education system and more like a self-help book. With nods to optimism, cautious though they may be, the final paragraphs, replete with a you-can-do-it attitude, end with the call to be more focused—don't try to be everything to everyone. The authors explain, for example, that their "optimism flows from personal experiences in higher education that can't be quantified but are powerfully felt" and that "the world desperately needs its university communities [because they] can and should be its teachers and meaning makers." Of course, such influence requires change: "Those communities that commit to real innovation, to changing their DNA from the inside out, may find extraordinary rewards."[18] This approach to disruption, one that advocates a shift to online education, represents the restricted context of BYU-Idaho, but is generalized to all of higher education. Only by reading the fine print will readers find that their results may vary. The final line of the book culminates the progression from the particular to the vacuously general. Speaking about higher education administrators who follow their self-help recommendations, the authors end by stating, "If they embrace innovation and give up the ambition to have it all, they can have much, much more."[19] More of what, one wonders?

Parting the Curtains

On one of my first trips to teach in Georgia Tech's Oxford Study Abroad Program, I arrived at my lodgings to discover a bowl of fruit. A tag attached to a strange specimen read, "Eat like an apple." Other faculty members had received the same fruit bowls with the same instructions. We laughed about the oddity of telling us how to eat this exotic fruit without telling us what exactly it was. None of us ever learned. We knew one thing for sure: it was not an apple. I hadn't thought about this experience for a long time until I began reading Richard DeMillo's *Abelard to Apple*. In its preface we learn, "This book should be read like a novel."[20] My first thought was that novels are fiction, and surely he didn't mean that. I wondered if I would know what to call it by the time I finished reading it, or if it would remain another mystery fruit.

Abelard to Apple is not fiction. It is not even a sustained narrative. However, throughout the book there is a clear sense that we are going to be able to separate neither the text from the writing of it, nor the writing of it from the personal narrative of the author. As early as the preface, DeMillo makes it clear that he needs to place the writing of the book in his own personal narrative, and to create an implicit understanding of this genre in his reader's mind, he makes a number of interesting rhetorical moves early on.

In the preface we learn that the book began as a five-page memo, "a simple essay that could be browsed and critiqued by colleagues."[21] Of course, memos are business texts usually detailing a required action, and, in fact, we learn that what DeMillo had to say would seem—according to him, at least—harsh to some of his colleagues. We also learn that he has spent much of his career as a professor and administrator; that academics talk mainly to each other and are insular; that his intention is to reach stakeholders in American higher education who are not involved directly; that he will shock colleagues when he "parts the curtain" on higher education; that despite his desire to expose the inner workings of the academic world, he has consulted extensively with colleagues about the issues; that he has "no recipes for success"; and that his framework will rely on an arc covering the vast period from Abelard's twelfth century to Apple Computer's twenty-first century. As is typical in books on the future of higher education, this one issues a dire warning about the state of universities, their questionable survival, and the perilousness of their journeys in a changing landscape—a landscape to which they absolutely must adapt. Much of this landscape will change because of technology.

Rhetorically speaking, the preface, not quite two pages in length, is packed with subtleties many readers will not consciously recognize, but which are meant to begin swaying opinion in certain directions. DeMillo first wishes to establish his place as both insider and outsider. This dual background establishes his credentials as a knowledgeable native guide to the academy, while allowing the nonacademic reader to identify with him as one of them. He explains that he has spent "much" of his career in the academy. In other words, he has spent some of it outside. Later we will learn that he has spent a great deal of time in the computing industry. One thing is implicitly hinted: there are things that need exposing, things that the insiders don't want you, the reader, to know, but which he, with one foot planted in the world outside, has the integrity and vision to reveal.

As an academic myself, I found this hint seductively drawing me in. What, I wondered, would I learn about the nefarious practices of my colleagues (not me, surely)? Promising to reveal the truth, even unwelcome facts, is a classic pathetic appeal. People love exposés. They thrill us with the prospect of offering privileged inside information—thereby stealing a march on our more complacent and ignorant colleagues. Conspiracy theories excite us like crime stories. They stoke our indignation about inefficiency, incompetence, and the victory (until now, that is) of self-interest over common sense. No wonder we are enjoined to read *Abelard to Apple* like a novel.

While DeMillo is explicit in his pronouncement that he has no specific pathways for success, he makes it very clear that his "story" will be, at the very least, a kind of allegory meant to teach us how some universities will find ways to survive, while others will perish.

Influential Friends

Acknowledgments are often meant to strengthen the writer's ethos—the way in which he wants readers to perceive him as an authority—by demonstrating his acquaintance with other figures in the field who may already be known to the reader. What begins as a simple thank-you from DeMillo to several specific people, allows him to spotlight a program that was initiated during his tenure as dean of the College of Computing at Georgia Tech, and he wants readers to appreciate his "'band of well-chosen professors' who were fearless in reimagining undergraduate education."[22] Then he acknowledges a number of his senior administrative contemporaries (former deans, a past provost, and a past president). Next he includes a short paragraph introducing his relationship with Tom Friedman—note the familiarity, not the "Thomas" that appears on the covers of Friedman's books, his bylines in the *New York Times,* or even on his personal web page. After talking about some colleagues, DeMillo begins naming some industry leaders—again usually by first name to indicate a close relationship.

It was particularly strange for me to read this section because I know many of the people at Georgia Tech whom he mentions—they are my colleagues, too. Rhetorically this creates another window into understanding, and while that doesn't affect the general reader, I will admit that it influences my analyses. Thus, whenever my analysis must focus on anything directly related to Georgia Tech, I will call attention to any possible bias I might have.

Finally, DeMillo's acknowledgments section changes rhetorical purpose. Ostensibly he wants to recognize Pierre Abelard, the twelfth-century monk who has helped inspire his narrative framework. We learn that little is known about Abelard, apart from his love affair with Héloïse. Abelard, DeMillo alerts the reader, "was one of a handful of thinkers who shaped Western ideas about education."[23] Yet it is a story about another Abelard that draws DeMillo's attention—one that comes from his career at Hewlett Packard (where he worked as the chief technology officer). "Abelard" and "Héloïse" were code words used within the C-suite to represent two companies in merger talks: Compaq and HP, respectively. DeMillo ascribes some symbolism to the fact that the Compaq CEO, Michael Capellas (a man) did not know about this, but that the HP CEO, Carly Fiorina (a woman) did—this asymmetry of knowledge is meant to predict the ultimate takeover of Compaq. That, at least, seems to be the purpose of this digression. Knowledge about medieval history is equated with power. DeMillo extends this inadequately explained allusion once more at the end of the acknowledgments section by explaining that even Abelard became an insular academic who thought himself uniquely important, a hubris DeMillo argues led to Abelard's downfall and should be "a moral lesson for us all."[24]

So what is this allusion? Possibly it is a reference to the fact that Abelard was castrated—a bizarrely tasteless reference when taken in conjunction with the reference to the Compaq CEO, who was to be rendered powerless by the takeover. However, the reason Abelard was castrated is one of the classic stories of unintended consequences, and DeMillo ignores this, because it does not fit his narrative conveniently. Abelard and Héloïse had an affair while he was her tutor. In preparation for their escape into a life together, Abelard arranges for Héloïse to enter a convent as a ploy until they can reunite. Her relatives misread this situation, thinking that Abelard is trying to hush up the relationship by confining Héloïse there. In retribution, they find Abelard and castrate him. Learning that she can never rejoin her lover, Héloïse chooses to remain in the convent. Thus, in trying to protect Héloïse's honor, her relatives do exactly what they thought Abelard was doing. There is one additional unintended consequence that DeMillo also does not reference: Héloïse herself becomes an influential scholar.

That DeMillo should acknowledge Abelard (but not Héloïse) as an inspiration is therefore strange and seemingly purposeless. Given that DeMillo's message is likely to resonate most strongly in sectors of higher education that emphasize STEM education, perhaps he wishes to bolster his authority with allusions to his colleagues in the humanities. But since Abelard is such a historical anchor in DeMillo's narrative, and even appears in the book's title, it is remarkable that he returns to the story only once more in the book, and nowhere explains its relevance. If a slogan-ready bookend were needed to symbolize the origins of education, one wonders why Abelard is accorded such primacy. Why not Socrates, after whom the Socratic method of learning through directed questioning is named, or Aristotle, whose school was named the Academy and whose writings influenced medieval education with such dogmatic fixity?

As I became embroiled in the daily business of designing and teaching my team's MOOC, First-Year Composition 2.0, these tropes echoed in the background, and I wondered whether they applied to me. Were we really a band of pioneers shaking up the academy, or were we jumping on a bandwagon? Were we really insiders, privileged with the knowledge of what needed to be changed and the resources to make this happen, or were we colonists in a distance education landscape who had much to learn from its current inhabitants? What did the rich experience of being there—actually teaching students en masse—reveal that the impoverished experience of merely promoting, exhorting, and proselytizing conveniently hides? Above all, if my account was also to be read like a novel, informed by my autobiographical background, what light would my experience as a nontraditional student, lifelong educator, creative writer, and literature professor shed on a conversation that had been dominated so far by senior administrators, management gurus, and journalists writing from a business and technology mindset? I was committed to balance, but it was a balance that needed to be redressed.

TWO

My Educational Journey

A Brief Interlude

Rarely has my life followed the straight and narrow path, so perhaps I should have expected nothing different from my career in the academy. One of the most prevalent stereotypes in American culture is that of the professor living in an ivory tower; I've only heard of such places. Portraying professors as pampered and impractical is a useful way of diminishing their work—work that is often misunderstood because they never seem to want to take any time to explain their personal relationship with education. For me, my personal story is what steered me down my academic path—a path that led me directly to this book. My experience of higher education, of education more generally, is, one might say, complicated. Unlike the usual assistant professor, I have been an active part of the Georgia Tech community for over twelve years, but my intense engagement with the larger academic community has been decades in the making.

My background in education is diverse. I was one of the better students throughout my K-12 experience, but I was never the smartest kid in class. I was not the class president or the valedictorian. I was not the most likely to succeed. I was, however, highly adaptable—comfortable in most situations because I grew up as an Army brat; attending ten schools in twelve years of primary education forces you to learn to adjust quickly to a variety of contexts and situations.

It is safe to say that very few people from my past would have guessed I would become a professor at Georgia Tech, including my immediate family and me. Since my parents grew up working class and didn't finish high school (each later got a GED), it is a small miracle that I made it to college at all.

Following an ill-conceived marriage at eighteen and the divorce that followed two years later, college was an impossibility for many years. I had bills to pay, so I had to focus on my job prospects. In my midtwenties, having worked my way up the corporate administrative ladder to become an executive assistant, I decided I might dip my toe into the higher education waters. I enrolled in a public speaking course at my local community college.

As a twenty-seven-year-old freshman, I wasn't like many of my fellow students. I was placed in the honors program, but I don't think my professors considered me particularly remarkable. A couple of them did, however, see potential, and that potential, they believed, would take me to graduate school. After I received my associate's degree (one that some colleagues tell me not to claim),[1] I transferred to a small, private, liberal arts college to finish my bachelor's degree. My experiences there were a little more traditional, but I had to work hard to be part of a community that wasn't accustomed to older students. One professor told me, "nontraditional students upset the balance," and suggested I find a nice, evening degree program to attend. Once I arrived in graduate school, no one thought of me as nontraditional, but my work experience often set me apart and brought administrative opportunities that many of my colleagues did not get. My master's degree and doctorate came from large, state universities—one in the South, one in the Midwest—and it was in these programs that I added "teacher" to my identities.

Over the last eighteen years, I have been just one of the 1.31 million American college instructors[2] who are mostly just average people trying to offer an excellent education to our students. I have taught as a graduate teaching assistant, a postdoctoral fellow, an adjunct professor, a full-time, non-tenure-line instructor, and as a tenure-line professor—all this and I've been the founding director of an innovative academic tutoring center. Along the way, I have learned a lot about higher education.

Teaching in the Machine

My MOOC journey began as many journeys do—in haste. Within hours of agreeing to take on the project, my co-principal investigator, Rebecca Burnett, and I began working on the proposal for First-Year Composition 2.0, which we submitted several days later. We waited less than a month. In November, we heard that we had been chosen for one of the ten grants from the Bill & Melinda Gates Foundation. The announcement made national news; Georgia Tech would be receiving three of the ten available grants, and none of these were in the disciplines for which we are most known: engineering and computer science. Instead, the Georgia Tech MOOCs would focus on first-year writing, physics, and psychology.

Because we knew that planning a course on such a new platform would take time, we had gambled on getting the grant—moving forward with course design immediately after submitting our proposal. Almost every day that year from late October to May, my team worked on our course design. During the regular workweek, various members of the team met daily. Some of us worked weekends, too. To say that the project was all-consuming would be only slightly hyperbolic. The course launched on May 27 and concluded on July 22—nearly a year after I'd agreed to teach it.

During part of the early planning period, October to December, I was also teaching a traditional technical writing course for computer science majors. These were the kind of students I thought would be predisposed to like the idea of a MOOC. When I told them about it, however, they balked. Because many of the first MOOCs were about computer science, these students had already explored some of the courses offered in that area. They were unimpressed. MOOCs, they told me, were fine for getting extra information, but not much more. I pointed out the flexibility of being able to take a class anywhere at any time. They, quite begrudgingly, said that while they complained about having to attend class, they wouldn't exchange that experience for an online one. At the end of the term, several of them wished me luck in the tone people use when they know luck will not come. One of them even extended his hand, as if to shake it; instead, he enveloped my hand in both of his, patting gently as he said, "I enjoyed this class." His look was somber, as if he was bidding me goodbye in a very final way. This was only one of many unsettling moments I would experience.

We learned early on that Rebecca and I (and colleagues from the other two Georgia Tech grants) were being demoted from the position of principal investigators on our projects. An administrator at Georgia Tech's Center for 21st Century Universities would oversee the three grants Georgia Tech faculty members received. In conjunction with that decision, we were also informed that any contact with Coursera, the platform we were compelled to use, needed to be vetted through C21U. Things were starting to feel very political.

Almost immediately, our team began to understand that we would not enjoy the usual kind of autonomy we had when we designed and delivered courses. Originally we had planned to record all our lectures ourselves—with the help of a videographer in our department, a decision that seemed reasonable when we heard that Tucker Balch had actually built a small recording studio in the basement of his home to record the lectures for his Computational Finance course. We were disabused of that idea quickly and told by C21U that we would have to record the videos in Georgia Tech's Professional Education Studio. In fact, almost all our grant money, $32,000 of the $50,000, was going to be sent to that unit to cover the production costs. Another $1,000 was directed to C21U for unspecified "administrative costs." We objected, because we had planned to use the money to pay the group of postdoctoral fellows who were working on the project with us. Our provost gave us an additional $10,000 to offset these unexpected expenses, leaving us with $27,000 to split among most of the nineteen-member team. Neither Rebecca nor I received a penny—nor did anyone who had a full-time staff position at Georgia Tech. For all those months of work, the postdocs received just under $2,000 each. To put that in context, if a postdoc teaches an extra course for us, one that usually requires approximately thirteen hours per week of their time, he or she is paid $5,000. And such courses only last sixteen weeks.

We were only a few days into the planning of the course when I realized I should write about the process as I went along. The buzz about MOOCs was growing, but no one was discussing the very real and practical issues involved in actually designing and delivering one. When I began writing about my MOOC experience in the *Chronicle of Higher Education*, some people, even some colleagues, accused me of being biased and jumping to early conclusions, saying I had made up my mind from the start that MOOCs are an ineffective innovation. On the other side, I had disciplinary colleagues who accused me of selling out. I learned quickly I couldn't please everyone.

I admit that I was skeptical when I first heard about MOOCs, and I was even more skeptical about such platforms being able to provide meaningful qualitative evaluation in courses like first-year writing. However, when I made the decision to participate in this experiment, I also checked my skepticism at the door. I was committed to being as objective as I possibly could be, given that this was the kind of research project in which I was both participant and observer.

It was my commitment to dispassionate investigation that made me want to write the series of process-based articles. I was aware from the sources I was reading (the sources everyone was reading) that the conversation was already polarized. Few people were privileged to teach the earliest MOOCs, so I felt obligated to share what I was learning. I wanted to convey as faithfully as possible, from a "work-a-day" perspective, what it was like to prepare and teach a MOOC. To remain objective, I learned, often served only to make both sides unhappy.

As I reread my articles today, I am struck by how tame they are. Nothing I said strikes me as inflammatory. The writing seems almost too matter-of-fact, but I am pleased that I maintained my ability to stay focused on process and not get caught up in the politics. That wasn't an easy thing to do.

The day my first article was published is one that I remember with great clarity. I had made no secret about the fact that I had contacted the *Chronicle of Higher Education* with an offer to write the series, and when we reached an agreement about the number of articles, and so on, I told my school chair, my dean, and the provost. My chair was extremely enthusiastic. My dean and the provost congratulated me on the agreement. I didn't tell anyone in C21U because I didn't officially report to anyone there. And that is where the excitement began.

I had just pulled into the parking lot at a local Whole Foods store when my mobile phone rang. On the other end of the line was an administrator from C21U. In fact, it was the person who was given the role of principal investigator over our grant after it was awarded, despite not being involved in our project in any other way. He was not happy. He was extremely concerned about the article, and said that I had put everyone in a difficult situation. According to him, the big problem was that the Gates Foundation, which was sponsoring our project, could not be named in an article without prior approval. He explained that as soon as he had seen the article he had called them to apologize. (Having since had conversations with people from the Gates

Foundation, I think they probably welcomed the publicity.) He chastised me, saying I had blindsided everyone and gone rogue, and that my behavior was unacceptable. I informed him that my superiors had known about the article. I explained that this was part of my research program—protected by academic freedom. He told me flatly that it was not research writing. We were at an impasse. I went inside to buy some bananas.

The next morning, I came in early for a meeting with my chair to discuss the situation. He assured me that everything was fine. We'd been talking for about ten minutes when my phone beeped to tell me I had an email. I glanced at the screen. The email was from our provost. The message was straightforward: "Call me," followed by his number. I looked at my chair, pushed my phone toward him, and said, "Shit! I think I just got myself fired."

Provost Bras was very kind when I phoned him. He wasn't angry, but he did want me to promise to make an appointment to meet with our vice president of Institute Communications. I agreed, but I still wasn't entirely sure what was going to happen. My chair went with me to the meeting with the communications team. The team assured me that they would not interfere with my academic freedom, but they wanted to see my future articles before they were published. Their team, not c21U, would take responsibility for contacting the Gates Foundation about any coming press. The layers were building.

The institute's communications team also encouraged me to go through a program designed to help faculty learn how to talk to the media. I was assigned a media relations specialist, whom I began calling my "handler," as my point of contact. Over the course of the next few months, I dutifully reported for training and got to know many of the people in our communications office. They got to know me, too. I liked them. And they liked the fact that I understood their role—to protect the institute. They asked for a few changes to my second article. I felt that pressure, but after a few tense email exchanges, we got through it. By the time the third piece was ready to submit, I had gained their trust. They understood my motives, and in a couple of small ways helped me be even more objective than I might have been. Despite the affection I have for all of them now, it was a difficult period for me. I spent a great deal of time looking over my shoulder—waiting for the other shoe to drop.

It took a few months, but eventually the other shoe did drop. I was in Oxford, England, teaching in one of Georgia Tech's summer abroad programs. Because our MOOC was delayed for a variety of circumstances, we had not launched in time for me to complete the project before beginning my summer courses. That meant I had to facilitate the MOOC from Oxford during the last couple of weeks. A few days after the MOOC ended, I received an email from someone at the State Higher Education Executive Officer Association asking if I would be willing to attend an annual policy conference to talk about my MOOC experiences. The coordinator explained that the conference planning committee members had been reading my articles and were impressed. I was flattered and agreed to attend. A week later I learned via an email that I would not be presenting alone. The other panelist would be Houston Davis, the executive vice chancellor and chief academic officer of the University System of Georgia. I was scared. It felt as if I was being set up. I phoned the coordinator and explained that this was feeling like a very dangerous thing for a junior professor to do. She promised that wasn't the case and organized some phone conversations to ease my fears. A few days after returning from England, I boarded a plane to Florida. Once again, I found everyone to be generous, kind, and keen to hear about my experience. I decided the best thing to do was simply to tell my story. It worked, and that has been my strategy ever since.

On Being a Composition Teacher

I have been teaching college composition courses since 2001. In many ways, teaching composition is difficult to explain to people, even for people who took a composition course. If you register for a course, for example, on the history of American jazz, you can easily imagine what the instructor might cover—even if you know only about one or two jazz musicians. You take for granted that you will learn about things you don't know about, but you will feel confident that you will be learning about American jazz musicians and the history of their musical genre. But if you register for a course on English composition, you might wonder what exactly *composition* means. Generally, a composition course teaches you to compose artifacts for the purpose of communicating ideas, but not every course covers the same material or uses the same approaches. Some courses might focus on classical argumentation strategies (rhetorical modes), while other courses might focus on writing for particular academic disciplines. Course goals will always include helping students become better communicators, and that usually includes writing and speaking, but a course could also include composition of visual artifacts, for example. Many composition courses are offered as two, semester-long, separate but related classes: Composition I and II. In the first semester, students often focus on writing from personal experience, while in the second semester, students learn to conduct research and write about the results. In both cases students study model examples and review work of their own and work by fellow students. The artifacts used as models can be almost anything, which makes explaining the details of a composition course more difficult than explaining some other subjects. In the United States, very few universities do not require some form of a composition course as part of their core curriculum.

Teaching composition means listening—a lot! Sometimes "listening" takes on the shape of reading, but I have to be attentive to what my students communicate and how they communicate. Because communication has cultural contexts, I also have to understand how communication changes. I have to learn new forms of media, and be willing to revise my courses to include new communication methods.

The unusual nature of composition courses was one of the reasons the Gates Foundation was eager to fund MOOC pilots in this area. The ubiquity of freshman composition was another, as was the need for students to learn good communication skills, no matter what their major course of study might be. Planning a MOOC in composition meant, as the saying goes, "working without a net."

Our MOOC used a model based on a Composition I course. Students didn't have to do research; they could complete assignments based on their own experiences. We used sample artifacts that were freely available on the Internet. There were three major components of the course: writing, visual analysis and/or creation, and oral presentation, and each component had a corresponding major assignment.

"Teaching" this course was very different for me, despite years of experience in a traditional classroom. I did not meet any of my students in person, which would have been a challenge, given that there were nearly twenty-two thousand of them. Instead of sitting in a circle in a small classroom discussing composition and constructing artifacts, I had to prerecord videos for the entire eight weeks of the course—plus a promotional video that launched before the course to encourage enrollment. Every single course resource had to be preplanned and placed on the course platform before we could begin the first session. Students had to learn to manage their own learning—asking the instructor took extra steps because they couldn't simply raise their hands in a classroom. My team and I had to monitor the discussion boards for our course twenty-four hours a day for the eight weeks the course ran. I couldn't personally evaluate students' assignments because there were so many students. Once a week we did interact with a small group of students in an online Google Hangout forum. These interactions best represented what I do in my traditional classes, and so for eight weeks, I felt glued to my computer screen.

This brings me to the composition of this book. Many educators who are drawn to the teaching of composition are writers themselves, and so any writing about composition teaching is necessarily reflexive. A book like this embodies the compositional choices that we teach our students to make, and the most important question for me was my dual role as agent and researcher. I was a teacher and sometimes a reluctant agent of change. But when looking over my own shoulder, musing about the broader significance of the events that were unfolding before me, the MOOC became an exemplar of trends in the evolution of higher education.

During the MOOC, when was I recording my experiences and observations and writing the blog posts for the *Chronicle of Higher Education*, I restricted myself to the immediate experience of preparing and teaching the course. I described; I did not explain or judge. In the intervening four years, though, I have gained distance from the experience and continued to participate in a national dialogue about technology in teaching, especially in the humanities. For this reason, I inject my experiences into the ensuing chapters, each of which deals with a specific theme that appears in arguments about the future of higher education. My concrete experience sometimes supports but more often refutes these arguments. I chose not to distance myself in a manner that is more common in scholarly writing in the humanities. A detached "view from nowhere" is given to very few of the writers who attempt it. Mine is a view from somewhere. It's a view from inside.

THREE

Sweet Disruption

Disruptive innovation is a theory of radical, transformative change in business environments. It differs from most business theories by concentrating on the dynamics of the change process when technology catalyzes upheavals in how a business sector is organized. Christensen developed the theory by looking at the history of certain business sectors.

Briefly, the dynamics of disruptive business innovations go like this: first, there must be an established and successful business sector that is filled with industry leaders who are comfortably secure with a reliable and satisfied customer base. These leaders have little motivation to innovate other than incrementally. Indeed, actively promoting radical innovations in their core business area may undercut their market leadership. For example, Kodak famously declined to invest heavily in digital cameras when they were still rudimentary, because film technology seemed at the time to have an unassailable advantage.

For disruptive innovation to occur, this complacency must be exploited by small organizations that infiltrate the market from below. With little to lose, small companies can court underserved customers. The market leaders do not see this as a threat because their market is almost completely unaffected. Gradually, however, and with increasing pace, the agile, innovative competitors develop improved versions of the technology that gave them entry into the market, and start to cut noticeably into the leaders' market share. Too late, the bigger organizations attempt to invest in the new ideas, but their organizational inertia, vested interests, and the time they need to spend playing catch-up count against their prospects of success. Within a few years, the landscape changes dramatically, and the formerly small and once irrelevant innovators have gained ascendancy.

The future of higher education, if it is vulnerable to disruptive innovation, could play out similarly. The higher education establishment, consisting of institutions that have been doing the same thing for decades, and in some cases centuries, takes it for granted that students will continue to come to be educated between the ages of eighteen and twenty-three. Despite the increasing costs of higher education and the development of a large nontraditional student "market" (the majority of undergraduates in the United States[1] are in, returning from, or rejected by the workforce, not coming straight from high school), most colleges and universities are unaware of or unresponsive to the changing environment. Meanwhile, for-profit institutions, MOOC platforms, alternative accreditation agencies that are lobbying for competency-based credentials, and the "unschooling" movement,[2] provide an ecosystem of agile competitors that the established institutions cannot afford to ignore.

Christensen is not without his critics. Some of the standard examples of disruptive innovation, they claim, are artifacts of cherry-picked historical data[3] or do not illustrate the phenomenon at all.[4] My purpose, though, is not to evaluate whether disruptive innovation is real or whether it will have dramatic effects on higher education; my goal is to analyze the discourse around higher education that has given the concept of disruption such currency.

Disruption appeals to the audience's desire to be in the vanguard. It is the antidote to complacency, and no one whose career revolves around the objectives of critical thinking and originality—the pillars of scholarship—wants to be accused of that. There is therefore a subtle shift in the burden of the argument in favor of disruptive change, as opposed to stasis. To argue in favor of disruptive innovations becomes the new status quo, and it is those who are skeptical who incur the burden of evidence.

Discussions of disruptive innovation frequently conflate "is" (or "will be") and "ought." In spite of these distinctions, however, writers often shift from making dire warnings to an apparently gleeful endorsement of disruption. This is not unrelated to the frequent use of millenarian or religiously toned language, which often warns against a coming apocalypse and embraces disruption as a cleansing force.

Something that Christensen and his followers have not addressed is the sudden and disruptive effect of language independent of the disruptions being referred to. Perhaps this is because most of the businesses that have been studied in this way are about making and selling *things*. But education is an epistemic construct. What is being "sold" in the education "market" is the capacity to learn and act effectively in the world. So there is the possibility that disruption talk could have *illocutionary force,* that is, *talk* about the future becomes an *act* of warning that impels the very changes predicted.[5] If enough people constantly talk about disruption, the concepts being referred to and "sold" will become redefined, and the disruption will be interpreted as an imperative.

When the *New York Times* proclaimed 2012 to be the Year of the MOOC, the names of companies like Coursera and Udacity, followed quickly by EdX, began to be heralded as the most revolutionary thing to happen to education since Gutenberg gave us the printing press. In May 2013, Aaron Bady wrote in "The MOOC Moment and the End of Reform":

> The MOOC phenomenon is also a shift in discourse, a shift that's happened so quickly and so recently, that it fills up our mental rear-view mirror. When the word "MOOC" was first coined in 2008, by a set of Canadian academics who needed a term to describe the experiment in pedagogy they were putting together, the word itself was a niche term that most people in higher education would not hear about, or need to. In the last year, it's gone from a rather singular experiment in connectivist and distributed learning to a behemoth force that we are told and retold is reshaping the face of higher education. And whether MOOCs are disrupting education through innovation . . . or simply representing the disruption of education as it is embedded in the market, the phenomenon under discussion has changed quite dramatically as it has migrated from Canada to Silicon Valley.[6]

It is instructive how such appeals to disruption work on us. They are designed to scare us by analogy with other familiar threats, but they also speak to our better natures: educational disruption will be good for everyone, especially the underserved around the world.

The Rhetoric of Fear and Generosity

When DeMillo discusses Christensen's work in *Abelard to Apple,* he solidifies his stance that universities need to adapt corporate models and approaches to remain viable. Mere reform will be insufficient; they need to acquiesce to disruption. His language is thick with words that regularly describe business and industry, particularly those involving the radical changes in the transactions between suppliers and customers. What is at stake is nothing short of the survival of most institutions of higher education as we know them.

For example, DeMillo alerts readers that "the business model for American universities is under assault, virtually guaranteeing that prosperous twenty-first-century institutions are going to look and behave differently than their predecessors."[7] Readers are bombarded with words and phrases like "crisis," "financial meltdown," "urgent," "entrenched," and "danger." Language like this, both in the words chosen by DeMillo himself and appearing in the quotations he cites by other authors, are intended to attract attention, and then excite and alarm readers. Disruption advocates favor the employment of a rhetoric of fear to convince audiences that change is both urgently necessary and inevitable.

Readers often find the best examples of this kind of rhetoric in journalistic accounts. In the *New York Times* in 2013 Friedman argued that the "MOOCs revolution . . . is here and is real," and went on to comment about "how much today's traditional university has in common with General Motors of the 1960s, just before Toyota used a technology breakthrough to come from nowhere and topple G.M."[8] This kind of comparison has become commonplace. MOOCs are a "campus tsunami," to use Hennessy's[9] and columnist David Brooks's term,[10] one that we all need to pay attention to before we are swept away.

DeMillo contrasts this sense of urgency with the notion that universities are intransigent places where "it takes a lot to get us excited"[11]—an expression he links to a story about trying to pitch a software engineering course for a sabbatical visit to the University of Padua, Italy, in the early 1990s. By using this example, DeMillo not only positions the modern American university as a place where change is unlikely to be welcome but, by comparing it to one of the oldest universities in the world, he more strongly links a modern system to a much older tradition that, he argues, is even more conservative and risk-averse. This tactic increases the potency of descriptions that readers see throughout the book's lengthy discussions of the history of higher education—where we have the mysterious world of the academy revealed to us in its shocking reluctance to entertain change, even when its very existence is threatened: "The same curtain that uses symbolism and ceremony to cloak daily life in the university also casts its finances into shadow, an unfortunate combination for institutions that would benefit from openness and transparency."[12] Thus, DeMillo's careful choices of language serve not merely as a call to action against a common threat, but also as a way to position the disruption agenda as being on the side of the honestly curious as opposed to the smugly unaccountable. It is a rhetorical device that encourages readers to join the party of tomorrow and abandon any lingering allegiance to the party of yesterday. Incremental steps that start from where we are may not be a quick enough response when faced with agile competitors who are starting from scratch.

It is easy to understand why writers like DeMillo and Christensen and Eyring are widely cited. They tap into the frustration of those who point to the academy and say "we" are Luddites—and not completely without justification, especially in the humanities. As recently as 2001, I had professors in graduate school who refused to use email. Nevertheless, if you want to find a history of technology use driven by purely pedagogical goals, you need look no further than the humanities and those instructors who taught first-year writing in some of the first computer classrooms. As a graduate assistant at the University of Nebraska, I was one of the first people to volunteer to teach in a computer classroom. Muriel Harris, who recently retired from Purdue University, spent years doing research on writing centers and using the data to develop the first Online Writing Lab web resource. Ken Price was the first person to introduce me to the term *digital humanities* by way of his and Ed Folsom's extraordinary Whitman Digital Archive.[13] Many professors from other fields in the humanities (film studies, for one) have been integrating technology into their classroom practices for decades. For the most part, the average academic is curious enough to experiment with technology; but without evidence, an academic will not easily be convinced of any transformational outcomes facilitated by technology. What they are very unlikely to be moved by, however, is technology for its own sake.

One key to bringing more technology use into classrooms is to create training programs for faculty members. Often the most overarching problem is not a predisposition against using technology; rather, it's the time required to learn how to effectively integrate technology into one's teaching methods. At a place like Georgia Tech, time may be more readily available than in many universities. For a small school, where instructors teach five courses per term, there may be scant time to dedicate to such training—and that even if the technology is available.

Toward a Global Higher Education Economy

Turning to the global effects of disruption, and appeals to our generosity for those in the developing world, there is a clear political agenda at work. As Eric Spiegel, president and CEO of Siemens USA, says:

> Online education allows students around the world to learn from recognized leaders in higher education, regardless of where they live. Online courses, like MOOCs, are challenging the foundations of traditional education [sic] institutions. With the cost of college prohibitively high in the US and nearly half of our nation's youth unsure that their college education has improved their chances of finding a job . . . access to free online courses provides another avenue for students and the unemployed to acquire and/or upgrade their skills as they look for employment.[14]

Despite its naïveté, this is a common form of argument about MOOCs. Who wouldn't want to help people around the world? More important, who wouldn't want to help people in the United States who would otherwise be unable to afford an education? MOOCs are provided as a solution to this problem because they provide easy access to hitherto unavailable educational resources. But the entire argument is predicated on the notion that people actually have access and educational preparation. It also presumes that they want to learn exactly what we think they should know.

Most of the innovations that are "disrupting" higher education come from Silicon Valley, where technology access and the desire to promote aid to the developing world are in abundance. But another feature of the Silicon Valley rhetorical milieu is a deep-rooted libertarianism that opposes regulation in favor of innovation. MOOC apologists would do well to consider the current situation with for-profit schools that are more entrenched, less agile, and less innovative than they are, but were also touted as disruptors.

Corinthian Colleges, a large, for-profit organization of various colleges in several states, announced its sudden closure in 2015, after earlier having been forced to close several campuses. The remaining twenty-eight campuses enrolled nearly sixteen thousand students, who "took out at least $56 million in federal loans during the last six months."[15] That is $2 million per campus, or $3,500 per student, on average, despite the fact that the entire enterprise was about to be dissolved.

Corinthian was quick to blame the decision to immediately close what was left of their campuses on federal and state regulators who prevented them from being able to seal negotiations with potential buyers. According to *Inside Higher Ed*, "California Attorney General Kamala Harris, who is suing Corinthian for predatory practices, has declined to waive legal liability for any new owners of the company's campuses"—terms any new owners certainly would not accept. Corinthian was allowed to continue operations for so long because the authorities knew that "wiping out large swaths of federal loans" was going to be problem.[16]

Explaining by Appealing to the Familiar

As part of my series about designing and teaching a MOOC, I was struck that proponents and critics alike were trying to define MOOCs in ways that everyone could understand. People commonly approach new problems by beginning with what they already know, and many early attempts at describing something new are often rooted in metaphors, analogies, and clichés about reinventing wheels or building better mousetraps. However, MOOCs were not like the existing structures we knew—neither traditional lecture courses nor traditional distance learning models. Massiveness changed every aspect of what we were attempting to do as educators and required innovative approaches.[17]

For Composition 2.0, this was especially true. When support technologies are rapidly evolving, it is easy to mistake the *pace* of change for a desirable *trajectory*, and thereby overestimate the suitability of available tools. Ultimately, my team found that we were not able to adapt our course for massive audiences in all the ways necessary to provide an experience like the traditional courses I teach. Yet given the rapid pace of MOOC development at the time, it should have been no surprise that there would be problems. In defense of all the universities that signed on to create MOOCs, I don't think any institution was, or could be, fully ready for these new platforms because there were so many unknowns. As a colleague of mine said at the time, "We can't build the track fast enough for this train to run on." And that was when eagerness and naïveté really caught up with me—I signed on to our project assuming that the track was already there. It wasn't, and that meant a series of disruptions.[18]

When I originally wrote about the earliest stages of our MOOC design, I deliberately used the expression "a series of disruptions"—the word disruption being chosen for its more destructive connotations. The rush to implement any new technology without careful consideration of the potential outcomes is risky in ways that for-profit business may embrace, but that some sectors should carefully weigh against the human costs.

A Numbers Game

Explaining the *new* in terms of the familiar is not restricted to disruptive technologies themselves, but also their effects and the social trends that require us to take them seriously. Having recently gone through a major recession in the 2000s fueled by a housing bubble, and remembering the Internet bubble of the late 1990s, any American audience is likely to be receptive to calls for change in new and different areas where there is evidence of an expanding bubble. Speaking of the mission creep of the modern university and the resulting effect on tuition and fees, DeMillo raises the specter that the high-tuition enrollment bubble in not-for-profit institutions will soon burst: "These programs may give students and alumni more than they need; because there is always a shared cost across the university, they may ultimately cost more than students are willing to pay for. When students stop paying tuition, the bubble can quickly collapse."[19]

Analogies also figure in his case that the Internet will be a "game-changer" in education. DeMillo uses the analogy of television stations and YouTube, explaining how difficult and expensive it has been historically to start a television network. However, cable television and the Internet created the ability to start new networks to reach specialized audiences. Much could be said about the role of regulation in creating new television networks compared to the Internet. What DeMillo doesn't say is that regulation is a key component of why creating a new television network was difficult. He also doesn't note that those regulations soon became an issue for cable networks, albeit somewhat different from the regulations imposed on mainstream (free) networks. At the time he wrote his book, it was still true that a YouTube channel offered much freedom—freedom that has since been increasingly diminished. In fact, the recent push by some to "regulate the Internet" has really been about privatizing the commons, giving even more control over the availability of content and services to what would likely become a select few. As Lawrence Lessig argues, "To the extent the architecture gets built to reestablish the power to control distribution, and thereby innovation, it is a constraint that is not demanded by economics. It is a constraint that simply favors some interests over others."[20]

Content on the Internet is likewise changing. More and more, quality information and services require payment or come with advertising. In the case of some sites, like *Wikipedia,* users donate money to keep the service operating, something a site cannot always rely upon for long-term sustainability. Additionally, the content on sites is becoming more regulated. Copyright, for one example, wasn't of huge concern in the beginning of the Internet, when the prevailing opinion was that "information wants to be free,"[21] but now authors are working hard to protect their interests. Soon, perhaps, they will be joined by teachers of online courses.

DeMillo's turn toward the "entrepreneurial model" has become a predictable rhetorical move—one that continues to make the implicit argument that universities need to function like businesses. "The rush to define the twenty-first-century university is driven by a combination of political and economic factors. It is fueled, above all, by *enabling technology curves,* the growth-driven law of the Internet era that describes the annual doubling of capability and capacity for equal costs. Paradoxically, mainstream universities—where much of the technology originated—have been slow to embrace these technologies, even as they became ubiquitous in other sectors of the economy."[22] Two things are striking about this passage. First, there is the idea that universities should become dedicated to the goal of doubling their capacity, which, in the case of a university, means doubling its number of students. If we think of students as customers (if, indeed, we should), then we must also consider how students are different from other kinds of customers. There are few customer services that require so much constant attention as the student-faculty relationship. To avoid reducing the *epistemic* capacity of the faculty-student relationship (for which student-faculty ratio is the conventional proxy measure), increasing capacity in DeMillo's scenario would require increasing the number of faculty members to serve the students. This is definitely not what he means. The only way to increase capacity, then, is by *reducing* student-faculty interaction.

Another idea introduced by DeMillo is that universities resist using technology that could solve some of the capacity problems, and this makes them different from other sectors of the economy. The implicit argument is that other sectors have used technology to increase capacity. Perhaps universities are resistant because technology has yet to create suitable ways to offer instruction that would allow something as significant as a doubling of the student body. In addition, universities have different incentives for the work they do. Traditional universities, even those which offer distance education alternatives, are not-for-profit institutions that do not have shareholders who expect dividends each year. To be required to graduate students is a very different kind of goal from the pursuit of an exceptional bottom-line profit—one that requires a great amount of person-to-person work. Unsurprisingly, for-profit institutions have very low graduation rates. Without regulation or active consumer education, graduation rates do not matter to them as much as other measures. And for a MOOC provider the carrot of a participation certificate is merely a way to monetize participation, not to meaningfully increase completion rates.

Rush to the Bottom

If rising tuition is a problem, so too is the expectation many people have that education should be free, or nearly free. DeMillo, Christensen, Eyring, and others invoke the idea of disruption to claim that greater technology will radically shift higher education's cost equation. The argument, in outline, is that by getting rid of expensive professors, going online, and acquiring online course content from the elite tier of universities, middle-ranked universities could survive and continue providing a quality education for their students. What is seldom discussed is the cost shifting that takes place. Just because an institution is not paying a professor does not mean that it is not paying other professionals—often a team of highly specialized and well-paid technologists.

Rarely is anything of value truly free and open. There are costs, even if they are not immediately apparent. A new industry must evolve to support the production and delivery of MOOCs. As I mentioned, production costs for videography and course design specific to Coursera (what I call the "Courser-afication" of materials) for our MOOC was approximately $32,000, covered in our case by a grant from the Gates Foundation. The balance of our funding ($18,000 from the grant, plus another $10,000 of internal funding from Georgia Tech) was divided between the postdoctoral fellows who worked on the project. The fact that neither I nor my co-PI, Dr. Burnett, received any additional pay is something that wouldn't be acceptable to many faculty, especially given the huge time commitment.

Many people do not understand that a MOOC requires far more time to prepare and execute than a traditional course. To prepare the three lectures offered in a single week, our team spent about twenty hours planning and developing content. I spent an additional eight hours rehearsing my lectures. It took just under four hours to record videos for three formal lectures (one week's worth). Another unit at Georgia Tech did the editing work and submitted it to Coursera for approval, which usually took five to ten days. Once we received the edited video content, there was more work to incorporate quiz links or other "in-class work" that took place during the video lecture pauses. Finally, there was the "Courserafication" process of uploading and configuring the content for use on the Coursera site. Formatting assignments and other content took still more time.[23]

All this setup work happens before a course begins. Once the course is "live," students expect 24/7 monitoring and quick responses to their queries, questions, and comments. If there is a problem, instructors must address it quickly—they do not have the luxury of waiting until the next class meeting as they do in traditional courses. For nine months, our entire team was thoroughly bound to the course—some of us felt these ties for months after the course ended.

As we gain more experience in online education, we will recalibrate these budgetary issues. Indeed, Georgia Tech faculty members who teach the online master's degree in computer science now receive a generous stipend that recognizes the significant investment of effort that their course design and teaching require. Not only that, but they receive releases from service responsibilities that must then be taken on by their colleagues whose course preparation and teaching responsibilities do not take place online and are therefore arguably less cost-effective.

In the early days of MOOCs, there was much talk of their being "experiments," although, since true experiments are designed to test well-defined hypotheses, it would be more accurate to say that they were a way for institutions to put their toes in the water. Once these gestures became full-fledged experiments and pilots, the issue arose: What are they for? What is the advantage to the institution that invests in producing a MOOC? What are its relationships with its students? Will there be a payoff for anyone involved?

In "The Hidden Costs of MOOCs," I note that there have been many "times I've chosen a particular restaurant because of a buy-one-get-one-free offer. And yes, sometimes I even return to the restaurant if I like the food and the service."[24] Special offers, or in the case of MOOCs, free offers, do attract a new clientele or bring back former customers who have dropped away. Any business that relies exclusively on such loss leaders and free gifts is bound to fail eventually, and this is the rub for MOOC providers. Some elite institutions can afford to continue to give away their courses (even accredited ones) for a time. They may recoup their costs in several ways. A diffuse sense of goodwill and buzz may increase their institutional prominence for a time, especially if they are early adopters in a small field, or their offerings continue to stand out once the field starts to expand. They may regard MOOCs as a pedagogical investment, with the payoffs coming back to their own tuition-paying students in the form of better "hybrid," "blended," or "flipped" classroom experiences. But this is a dangerous game. There is no evidence yet that if there are any benefits, these benefits outweigh the costs.

A more likely benefit arises when the number of MOOC providers shrinks or becomes stratified into an elite tier and also-rans, with the former category able to introduce entrance fees or tuition once their competitors have withdrawn. This is already happening. Coursera has introduced certificates, and the American Council on Education has endorsed the quality of some MOOC courses for college credit. Ironically, many early providers have not stood by their MOOCs for college credit, but students at other institutions could receive credit for them. These same students could conceivably later transfer from one of the provider institutions and receive transfer credit for the very courses that would not have counted at their new university if they had been students there when they took them. Certainly such a scenario will represent losses to schools that cannot compete and can become players in the MOOC ecosystem only by consuming courses produced by other, more elite institutions. San Jose State University attempted to take on this role, with Harvard providing some of its philosophy courses, with the local philosophy faculty taking on the role of tutors and (essentially) teaching assistants.[25]

Being forced into the role of MOOC consumers represents an existential threat of the kind that disruption advocates warn us of. It is an example of the widespread practice throughout business of "outsourcing" services to cheaper providers. In such situations, fewer faculty members will be needed to teach the courses locally. And if, in the worst case, a school closes, there will be the obvious loss of employment for everyone associated with the school—from the administrators to the faculty to the support staff. If that school is a rural or underpopulated area, the negative economic effects will cascade into the general community. These losses are palpable. Graduate programs in midtier schools may no longer be able to support graduate students by offering them teaching assistantships as a way to finance their education. If assistantships disappear, graduate programs will wither. And even when outsourcing does not lead to the loss of existing positions, it is likely to result in the reduction of future opportunities. Where will all those graduate students go?

The Personal Touch

Technology is always at the forefront of arguments about disruptive innovation, and higher education is no exception. Technology, from the mills and looms of the early Industrial Revolution to the production lines of prewar Detroit, has effected dramatic efficiency improvements throughout the industrial age by introducing standardization and repeatability. It does so by reducing the avenues for personalization. As Henry Ford famously said, "Any customer can have a car painted any color that he wants so long as it is black."[26]

An education of value is a highly personalized experience, and authors like Christensen and Eyring are keen to defend the concept of disruption in higher education from the charge that individualized attention must be sacrificed. They marshal several arguments to support this defense.

According to them, the reason BYU-Idaho and Harvard have been successful in their different spheres of excellence has been their ability to provide personal attention to students. For Harvard this comes about through an elaborate house system with tutors and mentors to augment the classroom experience. For BYU-Idaho, this attention comes from the volunteer network of faculty, students, and devoted church members they are able to tap into. Such nontechnological aspects of an institution can dovetail with technological innovation in the "delivery" component of education. Such are the findings by Chambliss and Takacs in their in-depth, multiyear study of learning at Hamilton College, who argue, "Contemporary critics of higher education tend to talk as if skills, especially those readily measurable around the time of graduation, are the primary benefit of a college education. . . . The college is a particular institution with its own specific mix of results. As they graduate and leave college, students talk about three different kinds of positive results: skills, confidence, and relationships."[27] Online courses can undoubtedly help with the acquisition of *some* skills, and therefore confidence. But the relationships developed through campus life are much harder to replicate or even mimic online. It is true that some types of online communities do justify the label "community," but face-to-face interaction is something many students want from their college experience—despite their complaints about having to attend class. Students crave real, rather than virtual, relationships.

Another frequent argument is that our students, who are digital natives, really desire online courses. As I mentioned earlier, I often ran our MOOC design ideas by the students in my technical writing course for computer science majors. They would graciously answer my questions, but they were clear about one thing: this was not the way they wanted to get *their* education. When I challenged them, pointing out that they complained about coming to class and that they often consulted online sources for information, they agreed but said they still wouldn't want to give up the "in person" experience. For all the griping, they enjoyed the social aspects of class. They also appreciated having a personal relationship with me. One day I pressed them, "Couldn't we just use social media to connect?" A student responded, "If I reach out to you, I want help—not photos of what you had for dinner." As for consulting online sources, they agreed they did and they would continue to do so. However, they were savvy enough to know that some of that information needed a kind of curation—something they counted on me to provide.

Plus Ça Change, Except This Time

Given that we learn from DeMillo that the modern university contains a cloistered faculty that naturally wishes to protect its privileges, it is no surprise that he compares the impact of the MOOC movement to the problems faced by the Jesuits when moving type printing and the development of widespread literacy was becoming common among the growing middle class of burgers and merchants. DeMillo explains, "Textbooks were widely available, and it worried the Jesuits greatly that they had to find a way to be valuable beyond the rote memorization of what a distant scholar had written."[28]

The parallel between the Jesuits and the modern university is not a casual analogy. Throughout Part 3 of DeMillo's book, readers are treated with a succession of episodes from the history of universities that underscore his message that disruptive change is imperative. His chapter "The Value of a University" begins with an epigraph from John Henry Newman's 1899 *The Idea of a University*: "When a university has been doing *useless* things for a long time it appears at first degrading to them to be *useful*" [my emphasis].

Rhetorically speaking, this baits the reader. The epigraph clearly indicates that the coming arguments likely will paint universities in an unfavorable light. Once again readers are provided descriptions of the university as old-fashioned, outmoded, and too conservative to change: "Modern colleges and universities are essentially unchanged since medieval times."[29] How do we know this is true? According to DeMillo, because academics still wear regalia that takes its cues from the thirteenth century; because the administrative structures are the same as those "handed down intact from the masters at the University of Paris"; because our degree names (bachelor, master, doctor) remain the same; and because "the idea of curriculum—and even the name 'liberal arts'—comes directly from the required courses of study at the first universities in Europe."[30]

DeMillo supports his frustration about the inertia of modern academic institutions with historical analogies that, I suppose, he intends should illustrate the dangers of inaction. What is strange about his historical narrative, though, is that at least one of these lessons from history appears to do the opposite. Intransigent academics who do not want to join the modern world can take solace from the story that he tells. DeMillo explains that the Jesuits established their value by promising "preparation for professional life." Similarly, the Protestant churches began to form academies, too, filling a gap for students who repudiated Catholic doctrine. Meanwhile, the older master's guilds in the original Studia "reacted by circling the wagons . . . and [becoming] more conservative and protective of their profession."[31]

Thus, the era of Gutenberg was when the hegemony of the church and the guilds was shown to be little more than dogma and protectionism. Average people could or at least should have been able to make their own way. In modern terms, the universities and faculty unions were, like the medieval universities and guilds, holding people back and acting as self-appointed gatekeepers. One might therefore expect the alleged intransigence of church and guilds alike to cause them to be swept away by a "tsunami" of freethinking and trade conducted independently of the guilds, since that is what allegedly threatens today's academy. But of course the truth did not set the power echelons of a society free overnight; this happened only gradually over several centuries. Counterreformations and vested interests have great potential to resist and reverse change, and their supporters, by definition, have opinions, too. In fact, until the Industrial Revolution this method of protectionist foot-dragging worked for higher education. For several hundred years, English universities were mired in the teachings of the Scholastics and were largely unaffected in their curricula by Enlightenment advances.[32] It was not until the formation of the University of London at the turn of the nineteenth century that England had any university unaffiliated with the Church of England. Jews, nonconformists, and agnostics simply could not attend college unless they were prepared to swear an oath of allegiance to the Anglican faith.[33] Graduating from Cambridge in 1800, a gentleman would be likely to know much more about Aristotle than about Newton. And yet the late medieval and early modern university did not impede the development of technological advances: early engineering drove the development of scientific research, not the other way around.

None of this is to say that refusing to adapt is laudable. The denial of educational opportunities to masses of people for centuries is no cause for celebration. But it reminds us that "ought" does not imply "is." The need for radical change in today's universities—even if it is accepted that such change is desirable—does not imply that change will inevitably occur. To imply that because the church should have embraced the widespread publication of scripture, modern universities should also embrace the use of MOOCs is simply a weak analogy.

Beware of Geeks Bearing Gifts

Disruption advocates are correct that universities will begin to feel pressure to consider how technology reshapes their practices—ignoring these considerations could determine whether institutions survive. What they did not foresee was a group of professors at Stanford who were determined to develop an alternative to the modern university—one that some supporters believed could eliminate the need for most universities throughout the world, no matter how innovative they become.

The tone throughout *The Innovative University* is akin to that of a kind uncle giving stern advice. Christensen and Eyring give an admonition that "technological and social change threatens to undermine the traditional university's dominance,"[34] and that change will come quickly. However, they contend that the only danger faculty and staff face is in doing nothing.

Christensen and Eyring argue the inevitability of shifting courses online, but explain how this is easier to do than many people imagine, given that "traditional universities have all the assets needed to compete effectively in the online environment."[35] I wish this were true. I wonder how many small schools (especially ones in remote areas) they visited or consulted before proclaiming the wide availability of resources. Many small colleges do not have a wide range of technological assets, nor can they require incoming students to own a computer. As late as 2000, there was a sick joke at my alma mater,

Oglethorpe University, that if the "Unabomber" (Theodore Kaczynski), who disdained the dehumanizing adoption of technology, had become a faculty member there, rather than at Berkeley, no one would have ever died by his hand. Offering a single online course at such a college would necessitate a large investment in both technology and technology specialists, not to mention instructional designers and student support staff. No doubt this is the source of the fear felt by many faculty members at traditional universities when they hear statements like this: "The most powerful mechanism of cost reduction is online learning. All but the most prestigious institutions will effectively have to create a second, virtual university within the traditional."[36] For the faculty and administrators at some schools, any notion that they will necessarily have to convert to online platforms probably seems a very distant possibility because they are already highly specialized and serve a niche community of students. Even Christensen and Eyring recognize the special way in which small liberal arts universities function. One reason such institutions are successful is they are able to brand themselves with a certain level of prestige.[37] They cultivate a firm sense of "specialness" for their students, most of whom enjoy strong connections with their faculty mentors and with fellow students. As Christensen and Eyring observe throughout their argument for a new online model for higher education, competition depends on the ability to adapt in order to attract and graduate many more students using far less expensive means, but highly personalized student attention doesn't scale.

Very early in the progression of MOOC fervor, discussions began about how small schools could host MOOCs from an elite university as a substitute for their classes. The implication of this model was clear: the courses from the elite schools are superior to the ones offered locally. This kind of hype is easy to accept when it serves one's own interests. From the beginning, MOOCs were about branding for the institutions that offer them, and only a very select number of schools would be chosen as prestigious enough for this new way to "teach the world." As Ian Bogost argues:

> Institutions like mine are afraid of the present and the future yet drunk on the dream of being "elite" and willing to do anything to be seen in the right crowd making the hip choices.... Group membership is a key obsession of university

administration, and it's why they take systems like the *US News* rankings so seriously. Of course, all such structures are partly fictions we invent to structure our lives and society. The Ivy League isn't a natural law or a God-given lineage. In this respect, Coursera's clearly got the upper hand among institutions that fancy themselves elite: once they get a critical mass on board, the rest don't want to appear left behind.... I wish pundits would stop declaring that MOOCs are revolutionary when they are merely interesting.... What's a more measured reaction to the MOOC trend, then? Here's one: Coursera is marketing. Buying in associates an institution with a vague signal of futurism and reinvention, associates a purportedly "elite" institution with its elite brethren, and buys some time while the whole thing shakes out.[38]

I did not share this belief at the time, although I did have some suspicions that it would prove to be true. I certainly would not have taught a MOOC if I had believed in advance that MOOC platforms were nothing more than marketing tools. However, in interacting with some Coursera employees, I gradually became resigned to the realization that my optimism may have been misplaced. I was made continually aware how little they knew or cared about teaching. I am not a programmer, but I knew more from my introductory Python course about their world than they apparently did about mine. When they made claims that a modification or customization for my pedagogical needs was impossible to implement I astonished myself in being able to engage them in a technical debate. I realize that not all requests can be implemented or prioritized, but I came to recognize a common rhetorical smoke screen for anything they didn't want to do. It would always be preceded by an apology: "That's a really great idea. We really wish we could implement that. It's supercomplicated. We won't bore you with the details, but there simply isn't any way to make a program do what you are asking. So, go ahead and work with what we've given you. We're sure that'll be fine."

For example, our team was concerned about students who did not engage in peer review. Peer review is a requirement in almost all composition courses. The idea is that you learn to write by learning to edit yourself, and you learn to edit yourself by internalizing what you learn when you edit the writing of others and share your criticism with them. Thus peer review is as essential to writing as laboratory work is to physics. In most MOOCs, by contrast, peer review has peripheral value. Realistically, it is merely a convenient way to get students to "grade" each other's work in the absence of an army of teaching assistants. When I contacted Coursera to ask for help changing the penalty for nonparticipation in peer review (it was 20 percent by default and I wanted it to be 100 percent), the programmer said that it wasn't possible to change because it was "hard-coded in to the system." When I pressed and made it clear I understood that the parameter values passed to some function or other simply needed to be changed from 20 percent to a range of zero to 100 percent, he seemed surprised by my basic knowledge of programming. At that point, he finally confessed that making such a change was not a priority on his end. Essentially it wasn't worth making a small change for just one course. But for us, that small change was the difference between our philosophy of teaching, which was based in shared critique, and theirs, which was based in efficiency of transactions.

For all the outcry about educators needing to be open to innovation and change, I did not see flexibility reciprocated by our MOOC technology providers. I understand they have to make the best business choices; I don't begrudge their wanting to make a profit. What I found myself wanting most was a simple acknowledgment of their priorities. I also wanted the same respect when I was not able to make changes to my practices for their convenience, especially when such changes ran counter to good pedagogical principles, and I said so. I have a professional responsibility to my students. In exchange for piloting a course for any platform provider, I think it is reasonable for the provider to expect some criticism. There is no need for the smoke screen.

After the course ended, we were invited to meet with the Coursera software development team in California (at our own expense, we learned after we had accepted, so I participated via videoconference) to discuss the potential for future changes we felt were necessary for a successful course. We had a pleasant conversation, and they agreed that our concerns were valid. They made it clear they were not going to consider making the platform changes we needed, because it wasn't worth the investment of their resources to pursue them. I appreciated that they took the time to have a meeting with us, but in the end I was left wondering why exactly they wanted to meet. Since I had been writing frankly about my experiences with their platform, I concluded it was mostly a conscience-salving or public relations effort, to say at least they'd taken time to listen. It was marketing.

There is a conspicuous contrast between the early rhetoric and the reality we experienced. Initially, the MOOC pioneers gave the impression of being committed to an educational mission. Andrew Ng, cofounder of Coursera, and Sebastian Thrun, founder of Udacity, gave up tenured positions at Stanford University to pursue their entrepreneurial agendas (although Daphne Koller, the other Coursera founder, has not). It is therefore natural to ascribe to them the attitudes of "true believers": "'From what I can see, most of the ed-tech entrepreneurs are true believers,' Joshua M. Kim, director of digital learning initiatives at Dartmouth College, said in an email. 'They want to change education and improve learning. They think that they can catalyze educational change more quickly by building an ed-tech company rather than working for a college or a university.'"[39] I wanted to believe that this is true. Unfortunately, when my team was actually working with Coursera, I never once felt this. Perhaps the gulf between idealism and reality was just the passage of time between the company launch and the acknowledgment of economic constraints. Perhaps it was the gulf between the founders and the developers in the trenches. Whatever the reason, the answers we got to our questions were always about prioritizing their bottom line. It was a sad retreat from a noble ideal.

And yet matters do not need to be so emotionally adversarial or disruptive; there do exist learning environments being developed by and for educators. The work in "c-MOOCs" by scholars like George Siemmens and Stephen Downes offers a massive open online experience that focuses on building a community of participants without offering any credit or certificate. Essentially c-MOOCs are about a social connection through peer-to-peer interactions (along with a faculty curator or facilitator) that encourages autonomous learning. MOOCs, like the one I taught, which are more like management systems that focus on providing content, are, in contrast, referred to as "x-MOOCs."[40] And while it doesn't constitute a course with a sequential syllabus, the resources and interactive exercises that make up the newest online writing lab designed by a team led by Crystal Sands at Excelsior College is another wonderful massive open online learning environment.[41]

Those Who Can, Teach; Those Who Won't, Disrupt

During a writing retreat in 2014, I was sitting in at local diner having breakfast. I was watching a work crew across the road. It was a familiar scene, a couple of guys digging and hoisting and sweating—every minute or so was punctuated by each man wiping his forehead with the back of his forearm. Standing nearby, leaning against a truck was another man, distracted by his mobile device. Occasionally he'd walk over, stare into the hole, nod approval, and then return to the truck. Scenes like this have been the topic of many a joke, but the truth of the situation remains. There are those who watch and those who do.

My omelet arrived, and the Jim Croce song, "Bad, Bad Leroy Brown," came on the radio. Croce, who was the master of blue-collar narratives, began the tale of a man so feared that everyone gave him a wide berth. Leroy, however, allowed his sense of invulnerability to get the better of him. He began to make advances toward a beautiful woman, only to find himself facing off with her jealous husband. After the fight, Leroy looks like a "jigsaw puzzle with a couple of pieces gone." I sat there reflecting about all this in light of the many articles I have read about disruption. Maybe I was picking a fight and would lose some of my jigsaw pieces. When I looked out the window again, the supervisor was shaking his finger at the two men, both now inside a large hole. When he turned his back, one of the workers flipped the bird. It is natural for practitioners to react cynically when know-it-alls watch what others are doing, offer an opinion, and then return to more engaging pursuits—or when would-be revolutionaries pamphleteer the public from a safe distance behind the front lines.

Therefore, it is instructive to interrogate the expertise and experience of the leaders of the disruption revolution. Again I turn to the passage in *Abelard to Apple* where DeMillo cites his own experiences as a teacher. In arguing for his model of "capacity" and against the high-touch model of education that I defend, he explains that over a twenty-year period fewer than a hundred students ever sought help from him outside class. Apart from nineteen who were top students aspiring to graduate study, the students who sought help were struggling. He notes, "I suspect that my help was of little value to them. There may have been many more students who were helped by my teaching assistants or paid a tutor and did well enough to avoid scheduling a special appointment with me, but they did not substantially affect my workload."[42] This is an astonishing admission coming from a self-styled educational revolutionary.

Perhaps DeMillo's experiences in the classroom are the reason he feels that instructors do not play a critical role in student learning, since he claims to have made little difference beyond lectures, and yet he has had successful students. If what one is providing is a static lecture, along with the occasional clarification of a concept or problem in the lecture class, then it is possible, I suppose, that one's value as an instructor is minimal. But this is so foreign to my experience that I cannot offer an opinion. As I have only once taught a credit-bearing course with a teaching assistant, I can't judge whether I would consider myself a responsible teacher in a situation where I had no idea how well my teaching assistants or other support personnel were helping my students. I wouldn't boast about it, though.

As for Christensen's students' performance, that is not a matter of public record because Harvard is a private university and does not publish data relating to how students perform in specific courses. However, as a professor in the Harvard Business School, it is likely that his exposure to the student population is exclusively via the highly selective and rarefied air of the executive Harvard MBA program.

It is a travesty that the conversation about the reform or disruption of higher education is being driven by a small group of individuals who are buffered from exposure to a wide range of students, but who still claim to speak on their behalf and in their interests.

FOUR

Talking Business
in Higher Education

The Innovative University begins with a double entendre. "No one could doubt that US Education Secretary Margaret Spellings meant *business.*"[1] Business, indeed! Here is the lynchpin for so much of the rhetoric surrounding the need for innovation in higher education: *business.* With a business perspective come many associated concepts: the emphasis on the economics of profit and loss; the measurement of inputs, outputs, and efficiency; the forging of business alliances and deals; and a customer focus (and debates about who the customers are, and how to reach new ones). Above all, there are the dual glorification of competition and innovation, and an imperative to *beat* the opposition and get ahead.

Christensen and Eyring are referring to the Spelling Commission's Report[2] on higher education. They acknowledge that the use of the business-oriented language in the report inspired passionate pushback, and that many educators saw the report as a political attack on higher education, full of flawed analogies. However, they maintain that it highlighted some important failings: the "report's most serious indictments—that fewer US adults are completing post-high-school degrees; that the costs of attending college are rising faster than inflation; [and] that employers report hiring college graduates unprepared for the workplace."[3] The Spelling Commission is one of many reports and books that criticize the direction and leadership of higher education, especially when what clearly seems to be the most important outcome (what businesses want) is at stake.

On the one hand, the Spelling Commission claims that US universities and colleges are no longer producing the products (job-ready employees) that US industry and business demand. On the other hand, former dean of Harvard College Harry Lewis argues that institutions like Harvard have squandered their academic and moral authority as stewards of intellectual and cultural excellence, preferring to concentrate on market competitiveness and return on investment: "In the absence of any credible educational principles, money is increasingly the driving force of decisions in universities. Students' best interests get lip service, but profitable enterprises get attention."[4] Discussions of MOOCs, and technology in higher education more generally, are impossible to disentangle from debates about the role of higher education in the nation's economy and the role of higher education as a support for personal opportunity. My own MOOC experience was an education in the business ecosystem of higher education.

The Production Line

The canonical business organization is the factory, with tangible inputs and outputs, and physically transformative operations that go on inside the walls. Measurements can be made, and the efficiency of the business and its component operations easily assessed, at least in principle. It is no surprise, therefore, that the university can be recast as a metaphorical factory that transforms the raw material of incoming first-year students into packaged, employer-ready units. DeMillo is quite explicit in his use of this metaphor:

> Every aspect of academic life in America has been penetrated by the language and thought of the leaders who were the most influential people at the time that universities were trying to define themselves and find their footing. They happened also to be the leaders of an industrial expansion that would last for most of the twentieth century. It is no wonder that their concept of what a successful enterprise should be like was the one that prevailed. Under their influence, the modern American university was crafted to look like a factory. . . . But neither the items that were to be manufactured nor those who buy them had been decided.[5]

This passage appears to give the credit for the modern American university to captains of industry—perhaps to rhetorically entwine the two as a way to bolster arguments for applying business models to higher education. It also seems odd to think that universities in the 1950s had no sense of what they were "manufacturing." I suspect people in the academy at that time would say what people would today: our "product" is our students and the skills and knowledge they take with them upon graduation.

Of course, the danger in adopting the factory metaphor and objectifying students as raw materials or finished products is that people are not products. The metaphor offers a little resonance when the skills to be taught are routine. It is easy to add a line item on a résumé when a person has mastered a programming language or become a power user of a technical tool; it is far less clear when a person should list "critical thinking" or "close reading of texts." The Composition 2.0 MOOC was one of the few humanities general education courses that had been offered when we launched it, by comparison with the profusion of MOOCs from Coursera, Udacity, and EdX in specialized STEM subjects with very obvious—although probably short-term and brittle—career benefits.

Behind DeMillo's deliberate employment of the factory metaphor (a favorite metaphor of many critics of higher education) is a conceptual framework that makes reference to factory operations and terms throughout his book as a subliminal background texture. The word *factory* and its cognates appear 42 times throughout his book, and *manufacturing* and its cognates appear 31 times. *Produce* and *product* appear 112 times. The word *cost* occurs 193 times, and the words *price* or *pricing* 49 times. *Competition* and similar words occur 111 times. In contrast, *know* and its cognates (knowledge, etc.) occur only 189 times overall, *learn* and *learner* (and related words) 157 times. *Teach* and *instruct,* and their cognates occur 160 and 82 times, respectively. Clearly, cost, value, and efficiency are presented on a par with the educational mission of teaching students.

If a university wants to cut costs or, like a production line, increase its "throughput," then one of the most obvious strategies is to relocate some of its courses to cyberspace (a strategy not unlike "shipping jobs overseas" to countries that offer lower manufacturing costs, especially wages). Christensen and Eyring argue that one of the benefits of online education is the cost savings in instruction. Adjunct instructors, who are more likely to be employed to teach online course sections, are far cheaper to employ than tenure-track faculty, and there are economies of scale in increasing the size of online courses beyond the limits that a campus's buildings or class schedule would permit.

Traditional universities' overproduction of master's and PhD degree holders relative to their own needs for new faculty members has created a pool of qualified online instructors who are willing to work for a few thousand dollars per course. By contrast, a tenured professor who teaches four or five courses per year and has no outside research funding may cost ten times that amount, on a per course basis. The only way for such a professor to compete, costwise, is to teach hundreds of students at a time. . . . Adjunct instructors give the online educators two other advantages. Rather than receiving an annual salary, as full-time faculty at traditional universities do, online instructors are paid by the course. This means that the online university can match teaching supply to student demand—an instructor is hired, or contracted for, only when a class is likely to have enough students to generate an operating profit. Also, an online instructor's teaching performance is easily monitored, and an underperformer has no contractual right to further employment.[6]

Essentially Christensen and Eyring are proposing a kind of outsourcing, or at least an ultimatum: either full-time, tenured faculty must move their courses online and draw in more students, or they should be replaced by cheaper contingent labor. Also implicit in their assessment is that once tenured professors do move courses online, then a university will need far fewer tenured faculty members in the future. No matter the scenario, the outcome is the same: there will be many more unemployed or underemployed college teachers.

Such programs have proven attractive to legislators, and several states have created online degree programs that either parallel or feed into programs in state universities. In 2013, the Florida legislature created UF Online, a virtual counterpart to the University of Florida that offers a four-year bachelor's degree on Pearson's online education platform.[7] Western Governors University is a joint venture created by several states, offering online, competency-based degrees.[8] In 2016, the Texas State university system offered Freshman Year for Free, an online alternative to the residential freshman experience. Its courses are all offered on the EdX platform and follow curricula that feed into the College Board's college-level Advanced Placement exams.[9] Many students take courses in high school that prepare them for these exams, and they receive first-year course credits so that they can move directly to sophomore standing. However, the Texas program is aimed not at traditional-age college students coming straight from high school, but at nontraditional students, who will meet these requirements before actually coming to college for three years.

While the promise of free or greatly discounted education is appealing to many, even if it is only the first two years at a community college, it is important to remember that "free" is rarely free. Whether the school is traditional or online, there will still be costs both for physical resources and for personnel, and these costs need to be met by tuition or charitable donations. By late 2015, less than two years after announcing its joint project with Pearson for UF Online, the University of Florida canceled the agreement because too few out-of-state students were signing up, and those students' higher tuition was to have subsidized the system so that Florida residents could benefit.[10] The Texas State University's First Year for Free program depends on philanthropy to get it started. The generosity of EdX course providers (whose MOOCs will be used to educate other universities' students), and supplements paid by students to sit the College Board exams will qualify students for the residential phase of their degree programs.

The MOOC I taught was not intended to make money or to save incoming students any money. It was an experiment to answer the question of whether a first-year writing course could be taught effectively on a MOOC platform. Our team never considered it a credit-bearing course. Nevertheless, we did get a request from Coursera asking us to allow for certification of the course, which involved students' paying a fee to receive a special certificate from Coursera showing that the students had satisfactorily completed the course. Our team declined this option because it seemed contrary to the terms of our grant, which specified that everything about our course should be free to the students. Coursera was aware of our grant but was, understandably from a business standpoint, looking for ways to monetize courses.

A critical problem with trying to apply business models to education, especially to public sector education, is that universities are not in the business of making a profit. Of course, that doesn't mean they don't have expenses. In the case of MOOCs, many of those expenses are shifted from a single professor (along with low-paid teaching assistants in some disciplines) to a professor and a group of highly skilled (and well-paid) technologists. Therefore, the costs of producing a MOOC can be surprisingly high. As I mentioned earlier, when we made our MOOC we were charged nearly $35,000 (at the time, half my annual salary as an assistant professor) for production costs. The true cost was probably even higher. We heard, quietly, from some of the production staff that they were absorbing some additional costs because this was an important project. Besides me and the eighteen other people on our immediate team who planned and worked behind the scenes (including another full-time faculty member), there were at least seven technology specialists who handled production for our MOOC.

The high production standards that students expect online mean that errors, or even minor changes to course content, require filming the relevant segments again—meaning that the technology costs rise in new ways. In a normal class, none of this overhead is necessary. Offline, I would be the only person paid to teach a class (it is extremely rare to find any teaching assistants in my discipline), and, if any adjustments are needed, I could change my course design or materials myself.

Facilities costs for classroom use are another issue, but this is true for MOOCs too. You still need a physical space from which you can broadcast, and the specialized nature of such a space makes it more expensive than the average classroom, not to mention that the need to protect expensive equipment means that it might not be used as frequently. Indeed, a recent non-MOOC experiment with a new learning management system required me to use an experimental classroom run by C21U to teach a traditional literature course. This space is not listed anywhere in our catalog as a classroom, and during the first week of the term many students got lost finding it. I asked a technology assistant who was setting up the new system how often the classroom had been used in the past for classes, expecting the answer to be not often. "Never, as far as I know," he replied.

Ah, some would say, but there are economies of scale. In a MOOC you have thousands of students. Yes, nearly twenty-two thousand, in the case of Composition 2.0, but many were just "grazing." The MOOC was free, of course. When MOOC-like courses begin having fees, students will expect much more from the experience, which entails additional costs. As it was, if our students weren't happy about something we were providing, they had few grounds for complaint as consumers. Yet that did not stop them from raising objections. And when they did complain, they expected us to address their concerns immediately. When MOOCs charge tuition, any complaints will be more insistent, and those complaints will be as massive as the enrollments.

Measuring Educational Efficiency and Quality

Efficiency arguments invariably lead to criticisms of university labor costs. DeMillo follows suit, explaining that in addition to the cost of a professor's time, there are support personnel costs as well: "The more attention a student needs, the more professionals are required."[11] An online environment will not eliminate students who need special attention; in fact, transferring support online will have additional technology costs.

Efficiency is easily touted as a reason for eliminating some fees. For example, DeMillo argues against conventional fee structures that are based on fixed pricing and that build in support for all students, even for those who do not require additional support. This, he claims, is unfair because only exceptional students (good or bad) require this additional support. He proposes a model in which students pay for what they use, because "exceptional students . . . are rare."[12] I assume this means that students always know if and when they need extra help, and having a standby group of support professionals will be feasible. Pay-as-you-go service fees could even become a deterrent when students discover they need support but haven't budgeted for it, creating a greater likelihood of failure which will result in repeat tuition costs later. Nevertheless, it is a standard conservative argument in favor of pay-as-you-go services that casts fixed pricing schemes, with their built-in economies of scale and opportunity, as burdensome taxes on the undeserving.

Discussions about cost cutting and efficiency are also used to question the value of accreditation of educational programs and institutions. DeMillo explores how accreditation plays a role in higher education today—a role he clearly feels is too cumbersome and expensive. We learn that an institution like Stanford spends "almost eight cents of every tuition dollar on accrediting and compliance that offer little value to students," and that "not all of the world's universities carry this kind of baggage, and when there are abundant choices in higher education, nimble institutions are more competitive."[13]

Language like "baggage" and "little value to students" paint assessment and compliance as not worth what universities invest. DeMillo is not alone in this criticism. Accreditation and compliance authorities are easy targets, and in their earnestness and self-importance they can often overreach. For example, I once took a mandatory compliance training session about research ethics to be eligible to do research sponsored by certain government agencies. We discussed a case in which colleagues were studying how waiting room design might calm medical patients. For this study, the research team had not only to get Institutional Review Board (IRB) certification to protect the human subjects but, because there was an aquarium in the lab space, also to submit a request for Institutional Animal Care and Use Committee certification. The researchers had to prove they were doing no undue harm to the fish. The fish were not accidental features; their presence was the putatively calming influence the researchers were hypothesizing would benefit patients. We all had a good laugh, and we understood why the research team was frustrated by the additional paperwork and delays. Common sense, we concluded, should prevail. But common sense is prone to special pleading and self-deception. We then went on to discuss Zimbardo's infamous two-week Stanford Prison Experiment,[14] which was conducted before IRB certifications were mandated for academic research. In retrospect, this notorious study raises obvious ethical issues, and the psychological harm suffered by some of the subjects should have come as no surprise. Indeed, the Stanford Prison Experiment was one of the dramatic examples that led to important changes in the regulation of research practice. Such review may seem cumbersome, but it is often necessary to protect subjects from harm.

As for accreditation or educational assessment standards, saying that they have no value to students seems wrong on its face. For example, ten-yearly reaffirmations are time-consuming and costly—Georgia Tech spent nearly two years preparing for its 2015 Southern Association of Colleges and Schools reaccreditation, but such work allows for important reflection and planning that help improve the services we provide. Professional degrees in engineering, architecture, and the health professions are all accredited by professional agencies, and they gain prestige when they are. A college degree in civil or aeronautical engineering, for example, indicates to a prospective employer that the graduate has command of a universally acknowledged set of necessary skills. Not having the right education could result in catastrophic outcomes, as was the case in the early, unregulated, days of engineering.

Likewise, a MOOC certificate is not automatically an academic credential, and there is a need for some regulatory authority that can protect members of the public from assuming that it is. A free-form market economy in nonstandardized credentials would only lead to predatory and deceptive practices. This was one reason that the New York State attorney general required the online Trump "University" to stop advertising itself as a university.[15] That institutions in other countries do not engage in these assessment practices, making them more "nimble," is a stock argument for outsourcing, and has as little weight as arguments against other regulations that protect the public.

Determining Value

Measuring success in the classroom requires a mix of quantitative and qualitative methods. We assessed our own MOOC in numerous ways. The first, naturally, was simply to count participation. We had 21,934 students enrolled online, 14,771 of whom were active in the course. As a point of comparison, the largest course I had taught before had sixty-two students enrolled, all of whom were active. Our twenty-six lecture videos were viewed (online) 95,631 times. Students submitted work for evaluation 2,942 times, and completed 19,571 peer-assessments (the means by which their writing was evaluated). However, only 238 students received a completion certificate—meaning that they completed all assignments and received satisfactory scores. If we define success purely by the raw numbers, then our course was unequivocally unsuccessful. It was an "experiment" that failed.

But of course, that would be very shortsighted. We did learn some important pedagogical lessons: the success was the lessons we learned in designing and implementing the course. From a pedagogical perspective, no member of our team will ever approach course design without feeling the influence of our MOOC experience—leaving us especially interested in integrating new technologies into our traditional classes to allow for a more hybrid approach.[16]

But to talk about success is to take for granted that there are uncontested methods by which success can be measured. More deeply, it assumes that there are units of analysis, such as "concepts," that can be learned as individual nuggets and that these can be assigned to "lessons," "units," or "modules" of a "course." Underneath all talk of educational innovation and technology is the dominant but highly questionable paradigm of teaching as "content delivery."

In my writing and humanities courses, I have chosen discussion over "sage on the stage lecture" as my primary mode of instruction. Creative writing or a deep engagement with the novels of Jane Austen or the poetry of the American South is nothing like "content delivery." Leading discussions, which are necessarily unscripted, requires more of my time and my full engagement, but students tell me that it is more "nutritional," and even more "tasty." Judith Shapiro has drawn this analogy with wholesome eating and the "slow food" movement in her calls for "slow teaching": "In the most basic sense, it is the ability to focus, to pay attention, take time to learn, looking back at least as often as looking forward. Most of our students live in a noisy world of ongoing virtual connectedness, relentless activity, nonstop polytasking . . . Like the rest of us, they suffer from the fact that too much information is the equivalent of too little. Like the rest of us, they live in a world in which innovation is not simply admired, but fetishized."[17] Shapiro proposes that there might be some value in applying the concepts of the Slow Food Movement to teaching. Let's bring back what is readily available, sustainable, and actually good for us, she argues. This certainly speaks to the parts of teaching that happen outside the confines of the classroom and even outside the curriculum.

Often the most important and successful rhetorical lessons I teach students are the result of conversations about things that have nothing to do with "the business" of our course materials or methods, and they are not paying tuition to consult with me. For example, I remember a conversation I had after class with a gay student about his plans to come out to his parents by taking his boyfriend home for the holidays. Because of our rapport, he had pegged me as someone who would understand his situation, and he wanted my advice. Was I a teacher in this situation? A mentor? A friend? And then, as I was editing this book, the same young man, now an alumnus, texted me on a Saturday evening to ask my advice about jump-starting his car. These incidents are not typical of my teaching experience, but they are emblematic of what matters to me. In both cases I was teaching life lessons, but in neither was I the "instructor." It is quite impossible for such interactions—life-changing for the student, as the first one proved—to have occurred within the confines of a massive online course. A MOOC's emphasis on firmly articulated learning objectives, learning analytics, and the accumulation of competencies, microcredentials, or "badges" would squeeze out and delegitimize the intimacy of authentic teaching moments.

On a lighter note, I once shared an elaborate rhetorical lesson as the result of a conversation about doing laundry. The conversation grew from my simple set of instructions about presorting whites and colors into a discussion of the "representations of domesticity for modern women" (my student's friends had been mocking her because she didn't know how to do laundry, something they thought all women should instinctively know). We also talked about socioeconomic issues (she argued she was progressive because she hadn't learned to do laundry, but had never considered that the reason she didn't learn was because her family's maid did that work).

Conversations like these happen precisely because there are one-on-one, face-to-face relationships that allow for more than a simple answer to a question, and these lessons offer much more than information transfer or content delivery in a classroom.

Business Alliances and Academic Life

MOOCs probably would not have gained traction so quickly if it hadn't been for the economic challenges that arose with the profound recession during the first decade of this century. Many legislatures took specific aim at public universities, believing them (and their faculty members) to have been profligate for decades. Turning universities into "sectors" created an easier shift to begin talking about universities in the same way people talk about businesses. MOOC providers, state systems of public universities, and ad hoc consortia of universities have combined their diverse interests into a complex online education ecosystem. College deans and department chairs were faced with difficult choices. Unsurprisingly, the response from some state legislatures was to create incentives for learning at scale or to mandate efficiencies. MOOC platforms came along at the perfect moment, as their designers were well aware: "Ms. Koller said she hoped the Senate bill would spark a nationwide discussion of how MOOCs could play a larger role to fill in gaps when colleges cannot offer enough courses to meet student demand.

Her company has had discussions with lawmakers in several states, she added. 'There is a lot of MOOC-related legislation that is being discussed in a lot of states,' said Ms. Koller."[18] For example, in Georgia, the university system has implemented a statewide general education platform, e-Core.[19] E-Core is being offered primarily for students in rural districts where local colleges cannot offer certain required courses or cannot offer a section at a time that is convenient for a nontraditional student who has work obligations.

The word "ecosystem" in the phrase "online education ecosystem" suggests that there are many participants who have unforeseen, indirect effects on each other. During our MOOC, we quickly discovered that we had to negotiate with unexpected outside constituencies. A representative from Coursera contacted all recipients of the Gates MOOC grants asking us to form a collaborative to discuss course design, which they expected to lead. While the offer was presented in the spirit of helpfulness, the implicit and intrusive message was that standardization across a series of independent projects was necessary.[20]

Consequently, we grumbled. As professional educators, didn't we have more experience of course design than Coursera? And should we care about Coursera's apparent desire to ensure some continuity of experience for its users across MOOCs? Why did it matter that students taking more than one MOOC on English composition should experience a similar look and feel? We wondered who would enroll in more than one course on the same subject, other than an educational researcher, perhaps. If students in our MOOC also enrolled in other courses, they would be in no different a situation than on-campus students who registered for courses from several different professors. As I said then, while all university instructors are subject to certain parameters, like requirements regarding the established course requirements, I have never had to consider conformity of delivery. If my institution does not enforce standardized approaches to pedagogy, why should a mere platform vendor do so?

As I discussed earlier, assessment is a key component of academic programs in every university. While we certainly expected to assess our MOOC experiment, we were surprised when we got a call from the Gates Foundation only two days before our course went live, notifying our team that we would have to participate in a webinar conducted by Quality Matters, an organization that provides subscription-based, quality assurance plans for online education. In watching the webinar, we learned about the company's program and course assessment rubric, a rubric designed for traditional distance education courses. When Quality Matters assessed our MOOC, we did not pass all their standards. Sometimes the criteria simply weren't appropriate for reviewing a MOOC. For example, there was no allowance for things we could not change—like some disabilities accommodations that the Coursera platform did not provide. This situation was different from the usual assessment demands, like those for our reaccreditation that were framed and evaluated by people from similar institutions.

As we attempted to manage these last-minute expectations and guidelines, we also found ourselves constantly trying to negotiate the technology within the platform. Joining forces with our peers from other institutions helped us overcome some shared technical problems. As I reported while making our MOOC, "collaboration is an important element. . . . the instructional designers of three other MOOCs devoted to composition that are being rolled out this spring have joined us to create a consortium to discuss best practices."[21] Collaborations also arose within my institution, not just with peers or others outside, especially when we needed IT help to coordinate our efforts with Coursera. Steadily, we watched as a new ecosystem began to take shape.

The notion of an ecosystem has also revised our concept of intellectual property ownership. Generally, an educator owns his or her course materials. As TyAnna Herrington explains, "Possibly the most notable disagreement to arise after the enactment of the Copyright Act of 1976 is that over the survival of the professor (or teacher) exception, which was generally applicable in cases decided under the 1909 act. The professor exception is a judicial creation that excepts the work of academics from work for hire status, despite determinations as to their status as employees under the law."[22] Herrington cites Lauren Lape's "Ownership of Copyrightable Works of University Professors: The Interplay between the Copyright Act and University Copyright Policies" to explain the details more clearly: "Section 26 of the Copyright Act of 1909 provides that the work author include the employer within the scope of the employee's duties. Under the language of the 1909 act, the works of professors could have been considered works for hire, but no court found this to be the case. In the two cases where this issue was considered directly, neither court found that professors produced work for hire."[23] In the MOOC context, I was to learn that things are no longer as clear-cut. In my traditional courses, I never once gave a passing thought to the question of who owns my course materials. Frankly, I would never have imagined anyone but my students wanting those materials—and in the case of a few students even that might be unlikely. When a course ends, I assume I am probably the only one who will be interested in those materials. With MOOC course materials, there are many additional elements to consider, including things like your likeness in video form and how "you" might be repackaged and redisseminated any way a platform provider chooses. With each new iteration of MOOCs (and other online platforms), the question of ownership gets increasingly more complicated. Even the courts and legislators are struggling to keep up and decide questions of ownership in a digital context.

My materials have remained in a kind of limbo since my MOOC ended. Recently I had to request access to my own course materials because the course information had been archived. In the place of my former materials was a shell for a same-named First-Year Composition 2.0 course in the new on-demand format Coursera is now promoting. What companies like Coursera might do with my course materials in the future remains a significant, and unanswered, question. I was provided access to the archived material within thirty-six hours, but a couple of months later I was informed that all the data would be further archived, and instructors would get some kind of data dump, although in what form I do not know. Even if Coursera acts responsibly, what happens if another company buys Coursera or executes a hostile takeover? What happens to the work students have uploaded to the platform? Universities and their legal teams need to constantly evaluate and reevaluate the terms of contracts with outside for-profit platform providers. They also need to work closely with faculty members who provide the content, to be sure everyone is protected in meaningful ways.

The Valorization of Competition

As the higher education "sector" has adopted a more businesslike mentality, it was inevitable that considerations of competition, rankings, and "winning" and "losing" would enter the discourse about education. What is striking, however, is the transformation from a mere acceptance that competition is a necessary adjunct to a business approach, into a glorification of competition as an end in itself. As if by the magic of Adam Smith's hidden hand, competition in all things will bring about improved quality and service to students and society. For example, Christensen and Eyring argue that the elective system, established by Harvard president Charles Eliot, refocused the importance of good teaching at Harvard: "Whereas past students had no advance knowledge of who would be teaching a given subject and no choice about the year in which to take it, now they could pick and choose according to preferred times and professors. In this way, the new elective system elevated teaching standards by market forces rather than by administrative fiat."[24] Economists accept that the flow of information affects the efficiency of markets, and when students are considered as consumers making consumer decisions, one has to take this into account. The reliability of the teaching reputations of the instructors that students choose, and the substantial lag time between these choices and the availability of feedback, makes the competitive market for choosing professors extremely inefficient. In contrast, when buying shampoo, a consumer is able to tune his or her choices about subsequent purchases on the basis of evidence at hand. In the case of MOOCs, where "enrollment" is a casual decision akin to grazing at a buffet, and discarding unwanted choices comes at no cost, competition becomes relevant when the reputations of the instructors are placed in competition.

Competition among academics over their reputations has a long history, of course. Perhaps the most famous interpersonal rivalry of this kind was that between Hegel and Schopenhauer for lecture audiences. Hegel, who already had an established reputation when Schopenhauer scheduled his lectures at the same time at the University of Berlin, won the battle, although history has yet to judge which of their systems of philosophy is the less obscure. And that, of course, is one problem when we consider students as consumers. Their judgments before, during, and even at the end of a course may not be as wise as those made with the benefit of long hindsight.

Competition suffuses discussions of "disruption" in higher education. Institutions still compete for students, and they publicize their successes in attracting the "best" students. Several publications (business magazines, interestingly) produce annual lists of "smartest" colleges. These are determined by various statistical manipulations of the SAT scores of incoming or enrolled students. According to *Business Insider,* Georgia Tech held the number one position on the "smartest public colleges in America" list for 2015.[25] I can personally attest that the improvement in academic preparation of our students has been professionally rewarding to me over the twelve years that I have been teaching there, and I am sure that the company of more brilliant students raises the standards and horizons of the less brilliant. As a public university, Georgia Tech bases its competitiveness in the rankings in its attractiveness to students from other states, but this is of scant consolation to the local students it formerly served who are not admitted. While there are many metrics used to admit students to a university, one of the key factors is SAT scores. In fact, universities routinely report the average SAT score for each new freshman cohort. Georgia Tech does not reject resident students who are better qualified than nonresident students. However, in light of the data for Georgia Tech's admitted fall 2015 freshman class (including those who were admitted in summer because they could matriculate as part of the fall cohort), with average SAT scores at 1445 for residents and at 1487 for nonresidents, it is clear that some resident applicants were not admitted in favor of stronger, nonresident applicants.

In fact, DeMillo's criticisms that "mainstream American colleges and universities do not know their competition today,"[26] and "no other modern enterprise has been as untouched by the changes in markets, demographics, and economies as the American institution of higher learning,"[27] are disingenuous. College recruitment campaigns are ever-present, even at small schools, with everyone rolling out the red carpet to attract a wide range of students. Whether it is the highlighting of a scholarship competition, the featuring of facilities, the workshops for parents, or the targeted population events, admissions personnel are keenly aware that they are "selling" their schools.

Increasingly, the entire university community is expected to be part of recruitment weekends. Even at Georgia Tech, a school that has no difficulty recruiting, faculty are asked to host potential students in their classes or meet with them in one-on-one conferences. Along with alumni, administrators, and current students, faculty members are also asked to attend social events with potential students and their parents. Many schools have armies of student workers who act as ambassadors, giving campus tours and phoning applicants. This intensive work begins each year in earnest, only days after the newest class of freshmen has been filled.

Students have gotten the "competition" message, and the best of them attempt to stand out, sometimes in the most formulaic and inauthentic ways—usually involving drive-by community service. After interviewing finalists for Georgia Tech's Stamps President's Scholars Program (a prestigious, merit-based scholarship program) I remarked to a colleague that very soon I expect some applicant to report that he or she had started a nonprofit while in the womb. Such résumé building is a fairly recent development. When I was in high school in the early 1980s, members of my peer group certainly wanted to do well, especially if they planned to apply for college, but I never sensed that we were already "professionalized" in our pursuit of the "next thing." My classmates who went to college held a certain elevated status, but which college they went to didn't seem to matter. I don't remember ever thinking or hearing about someone going to a state institution as being somehow less successful than a peer who went to one of the elite schools.

Competitiveness is also affecting how we design curricula and syllabi. Competency-based education, in which students are assessed by their all-or-nothing mastery of a set of competencies and acquire a collection of "badges" or microcredentials, is inherently competitive. Either you make the grade and can move on to something new, or you don't and must stay behind until you do. This is inappropriate to implement in the liberal arts, and it is an illusory approach to personal excellence that I have encountered in other spheres of teaching. When I became a yoga instructor while in graduate school, I began announcing at the beginning of each session that yoga is not a competitive sport. There is nothing worse than watching someone try to contort his body into a position he simply cannot yet manage. In fact, a person could spend decades practicing yoga and never manage to fully master a given posture. This is why it is called "practice," because there is *no* expectation of mastery—one always is moving toward greater mastery, but one must do so by focusing exclusively on what is happening now.

Universities that accept the disruption agenda risk becoming so focused on staying in a numbers-based race of their own making—contorting themselves, so to speak—that they will abandon the goal of education as the transformation of human potential.

FIVE

Welders, Not Philosophers

Nowhere is the desire to make universities more responsive to external needs and processes and to overcome internal inertia clearer than in the relationship between education and employability. Critics argue that, except in times of prosperity, students attach importance to a college education only insofar as it connects to their career ambitions. These ambitions will be more likely to be realized if graduates have a broad range of skills and perspectives that make them prepared for their third or fourth jobs and their second or third careers.

Jobs Training

Lurking in the background of the rhetoric about the economic benefits of higher education are the benefits to employers. From this perspective, lifelong learning and "learning to learn" have few benefits, because employers are hungry for entry-level employees. And when they complain that students are not ready for the workforce because they lack teamwork, leadership, or communication skills (so-called "soft skills" that are generally not taught in an organized and coherent way at college level), they are really asking universities to front-load their own employee training programs. This is the agenda behind calls for competency-based education, and this approach to education lends itself particularly well to technologies like MOOCs.

According to competency-based scorecards, the least obviously relevant academic disciplines are in the humanities and social sciences. For this reason, politicians regularly question their value. As President Obama said to an audience in Wisconsin in 2015 (a comment he soon retracted), "But I promise you, folks can make a lot more, potentially, with skilled manufacturing or the trades than they might with an art history degree."[1] And Rick Scott, the governor of Florida, said in 2011 that his state did not need more anthropologists. "I want that money to go to degrees where people can get jobs in this state," he explained.[2] In the November 10, 2015, Republican presidential debate, Marco Rubio argued, "Welders make more money than philosophers. We need more welders than philosophers." However, as Ollstein counters, the basic salary data prove that Rubio was wrong: "If Rubio wants to speak to a successful, high-earning philosophy major, he need look no further than his debate stage opponent Carly Fiorina, who graduated with a degree in philosophy from Stanford University, and went on to become the nation's first woman to lead a Fortune 500 company. Many other CEOs, hedge fund managers, and entrepreneurs hold philosophy degrees."[3] The mistake made in these comments is to equate a degree major with a profession. Art history majors are equipped to do many things in addition to being professional art historians, and anthropology majors do not need to despair if their degree does not open a career in anthropology. On the other hand, vocational degrees do not always transfer readily. If a hospitality management major decides not to work in the hotel or restaurant industry, or opportunities in that industry dry up—perhaps because of a glut of graduates with vocational training—then he or she could be worse off than the art historian or anthropologist who has broader, more transferable skills.

In fact, the often-maligned liberal arts major is proving to be more valuable than many people think. As reported in the 2015 *Forbes* article, "That 'Useless' Liberal Arts Degree Has Become Tech's Hottest Ticket," as more technology companies are turning to a model that embraces STEAM instead of STEM (the A for arts, added to the traditional science, technology, engineering, and math disciplines) to make their workforce more diverse and nimble.[4]

Even medical schools, as they continue to look to distinguish students who have similar math and science skills, are increasingly asking questions about the humanities backgrounds of applicants. Each year, I get a few former undergraduate students, usually biochemistry or biomedical engineering majors, who are applying to medical school and desperately need someone to write a recommendation that addresses their humanities background. Often I haven't seen these students since their first year in college. I tell them that my letter will be lukewarm, at best, but they beg, saying, "You are the only professor I can ask."

American colleges and universities have a model that teaches broad intellectual and meta-cognitive skills through general education, with the promise that an enthusiastic and self-motivated stance toward subject matter will lead to deeper (and therefore, paradoxically, more practically relevant) learning than compulsory courses with short-term objectives focused only on a particular job. Critics maintain that without some core general education requirements or elective courses, students would graduate sooner. Elective courses often suffer the most criticism. DeMillo explains how Charles Eliot introduced electives at Harvard after the Civil War by arguing for the need to move students to the center of university life, "not with an argument about what would best prepare a student for a career, but rather by arguing that students who select what interests them will pursue their studies with a passion that compulsion cannot match—a difficult proposition to oppose in a country whose Declaration of Independence was based on individual empowerment."[5]

Throughout the historical overview sections of his book, DeMillo argues continually, though usually through suggestion, that the European approach with a compulsory core curriculum and early specialization is completely disconnected from what students actually need to know for their careers. On the other hand, he seems, in this section, to be highlighting the American proclivity toward individualism and the right to make choices particular to one's own interests as a way that students can be motivated toward a "serious purpose."

The argument that students could graduate sooner without wasting time on elective courses may be true for some students in some degree programs, but there are many restrictions in the elective system in most universities, and upon closer review DeMillo's claim does not add up even in his own institution, where the number of electives can be very small, depending on the major. For example, for the academic year 2015–16 in Georgia Tech's College of Engineering, the number of free elective hours available to students majoring in materials science and engineering-structural and functional materials was 4 out of 132 required hours. That doesn't leave much in the way of choice or scholarship for its own sake. Perhaps these students would be better future engineers, not to mention citizens, if their degree programs were closer to the standard of 120 hours and they had more room in their curriculum to broaden their minds outside their narrow area of expertise.

Overall, there is the sense that students should have neither a fixed nor a flexible set of choices, because neither one is strictly focused on what a particular job might require. Again this fits the narrative that we need to train students for a particular career, not for the kind of well-rounded knowledge base and critical thinking skills that they can use to adapt to various opportunities throughout their lives.

It can be argued that an emphasis on the liberal arts, breadth, and critical thinking at the expense of vocational skills betrays an elitist perspective. Such pursuits are fine pastimes for the rich or the well connected for whom the traditional college years are a period of emotional maturation and network-building as much as skills-based education. The majority of students are not like this, however. They are "nontraditional" students, who come to college after several years in the workforce, not directly from high school. For these students, pressing economic needs (meaning the guarantee of gainful employment) are what really matter.

Many pundits accept this intellectually but do not identify with nontraditional students, ascribing to these students attitudes and preferences that are uninformed by direct experience. Worse, these writers patronize nontraditional students by projecting a set of unambitious and transactional motives onto them that they think such people should have. So let me set the record straight: I was a nontraditional student; I owned a home and commuted to campus an hour each way. When I filled up with gas on those trips, I wanted the cheapest and most convenient deal so that I could get on my way. I was a customer. When I went to class, I was improving, enriching and re-creating myself. I was a student.

If I had been starting college today, I might have been expected to want an online experience to save expenses and avoid complications to my personal life. I didn't. I gladly paid the same student fees as residential students, even though I couldn't benefit as fully from the programs and facilities I was supporting. Despite the fact that I stood out as different, I wanted, and I found ways, to avail myself of various co-curricular and extracurricular opportunities. I did not want an "efficient" delivery of content; I wanted the experience of being a student that I stupidly passed up when I left high school. Of course, I wanted my college experience to equip me for a better future, and in that sense it was a financial investment. But if it had been only that, I might have permitted others to advise me into a more vocational concentration, and would today be unhappily stuck in a well-enough-paying, but dead-end, middle management job. I would have saved money and had fewer loans to pay back. I have no regrets about passing up this comfortable yet constricted life as a white-collar welder. Fortunately, my two-year college offered a rigorous academic experience that stretched me to think more broadly about my future. While there, I certainly expected to be treated as a student first and a customer second, in large part because my faculty mentors, who understood more about education than today's pundits, demanded that of me.

Millions of students are in the same position. They deserve to be taken seriously.

What Do Faculty Know?

What we teach goes to the heart of faculty self-identity and the role of the university and its curriculum in students' subsequent success. DeMillo jokes that "nothing roils a university faculty like the question, 'What do our students need to know?'" because faculty "argue that there is [a] body of knowledge that needs to be preserved and shared, and that the price for calling oneself an educated person is to be steeped in it."[6] If an "educated person" needs some stock of cultural literacy, then this comes down to the content of the core curriculum of "general education," as opposed to specialized subject matter that is directed at workplace skills. In most universities there is a set of foundational courses, called general education. The importance of a comprehensive foundational education is crucial if we want to create learners who can become innovators themselves—an argument I made in an earlier article about general education.[7]

The benefits of a general education are best appreciated in the company of someone who did not obtain them. Often STEM majors can claim exemption from many of their humanities requirements, and while it is possible for a humanities major to be exempted from some math and science courses, it is far less common. In the case of technical colleges or certificate programs, students may never take courses outside those directly related to skills required for a specific job.

During my MOOC experience, I remember feeling most frustrated when I realized, one day, that I was on a conference call with a Coursera platform programmer about one of the changes to code we hoped to have implemented. My colleagues and I were trying to offer a better understanding of our request, and a member of our team said, "You probably had to do work like this in your freshman composition course." When the programmer told us he hadn't gone to college, we thought he was making a joke—maybe he was, but he never said otherwise. Let me pause to say that not attending college is a perfectly reasonable decision if you can get the job you want. In view of the glut of opportunities in computing, I suspect this young man didn't need a college degree to excel at the backroom craft of programming. However, as a systems designer interacting with customers and expert users, he needed the knowledge and wisdom to appreciate their perspectives, not a collection of certifications and badges in technical skills. A professional developer employed by an educational technology company designing a higher education platform requires context—such as a background in educational design, or at the very least the personal experience of having been a college student. It is, then, no surprise that many people who tout disruption wish to frame education exclusively in the context of the "delivery of content," a rhetorical choice that is particularly apt when dealing with MOOCs. A focus on the word "delivery" draws rhetorical strength from the language of industry and efficiency that advocates for disruption return to repeatedly. Delivery is about the process needed to produce more product—not necessarily a better product, simply more of it.

The Credentials Business

From the beginning of the MOOC mania, it has been unclear how platform vendors and "content producers" (that is, universities) would be able to "monetize" services that had been disseminated for free. One model was privileged access by employers to potential employees. Another was a standby of the Internet bubble: advertising and click-counting. There was the suspicion that what was offered free as a "teaser" would soon become available only for a fee (like the subscription model that some online newspaper editions have experimented with). But the clearest avenue for financial growth has been to associate the offering of a MOOC with the granting of certificates of achievement and completion. Students pay for these in advance, so certificates act as an incentive to complete the course. Certificates, it is claimed,[8] are useful as credentials in the job market. Employers may take credentials like CEUs (continuing education units) as indices of good faith efforts to become more educated or as a genuine warranty of accomplishment and skill. In the latter case, of course, the assessment of achievement becomes paramount. Mere participation and completion are not enough to demonstrate mastery of the subject matter, and any online assessments that really matter then become targets of cheating of various kinds.

In the case of Composition 2.0, the possibility of offering certificates engendered lively discussion. Our MOOC was one of four, and the teams that developed the four MOOCs regularly held videoconferences to deliberate over this and many other design and policy issues. All of us were asked if we wished to pursue accreditation for our courses. There were two formal routes to certification. The more academically viable was through the American Council on Education (ACE), which evaluates courses that offer actual transferable college credits. ACE is actively involved in the accreditation of prior learning assessment for job skills that obviate the need to learn an already mastered skill in a college course. Most of ACE's work at that point was therefore in the technical arena, not university-level general education. At the time, the details of how achievement could be proctored were unclear. For technical fields, one or more timed, proctored tests might have been sufficient to assess learning. For writing, however, continual assessment would have been needed. In collaboration with the other three consortium members, we decided to add an intention statement to our syllabus stating that our courses were not intended to be equivalent to a semester-long college composition course. I was personally unwilling to certify the writing of thousands of students with whom I did not have a meaningful relationship. Granting course credit would have been a disservice to both our tuition-paying students and those who enrolled in our MOOC. We were open to the possibility that a student might present work done as part of a MOOC to an admissions committee at a college, and we encouraged our online students to pursue such route if appropriate for them, but that process was outside our purview.

The second accreditation mechanism was Coursera's fee-based system,

"Signature Track," which Coursera uses to validate course completion. Without proctoring, this means very little. However, the main reason that we decided against applying for Signature Track validation was that we were working within a mandate that our content would be free to students for at least three years. While it is true that no one would be compelled to pay (the content itself would remain free), it seemed contrary to the spirit of the grant to offer a certification, or any other supplemental component, that only some students could afford.

In addition to these two forms of certification, a third "credential" exists that amounts to little more than a participation ribbon. These are the free certificates that are automatically sent to students who successfully complete all course requirements. These, too, are problematic, because gullible employers or admissions officers could mistake them for meaningful certificates. But what struck me was another issue that illustrates how unexplored some of the policy decisions around MOOCs are and how thoughtless are the responses of the technologists who make them.

During the enrollment period for our MOOC, one of our distance education staff members who was helping coordinate with Coursera asked me to send a high-resolution copy of my signature to be placed on all certificates of completion. I thought this would be a nice gesture, but wondered whether I really wanted thousands of strangers to have a copy of my signature. And even if the version of my signature was not electronically available to the students—merely subject to scanning, as would be the signature appearing on any personal letter—what about the people with administrative access to the site? Upon further investigation, I realized that fifty people had administrative access to our course site, thirty-eight of whom worked for Coursera. Of the remaining twelve, several were Georgia Tech colleagues only in name and were strangers to me. I wouldn't give even my closest, most trusted colleagues my credit card number unless really necessary, or my mother's maiden name, for that matter: Why should I give strangers access to my signature? It seemed bizarre to me that this had not been considered a security vulnerability.

At first I concluded that I was being paranoid, but I checked my intuitions with colleagues, including several who specialize in data security. Their response was unanimous: "You didn't give it to them, right?" I pushed my question through to our legal department, and they redirected me to the

Georgia Tech Research Corporation, which administers the institute's research contracts and business agreements. I never received a satisfactory resolution of the legal issues, but a week after the course ended, I got a message from another Georgia Tech coordinator suggesting that I simply provide a typed version of my name in an italicized font. It was an appropriate conclusion to a minor side issue: for something that looks a bit like a credential all that is needed to endorse it is something that looks a bit like a signature.

Some Things Aren't for Sale

When some students hear the message that they are *buying* an education, they can misinterpret this to mean that they are buying academic success and are entitled to the grades they want. With graduate students, contingent faculty, and junior faculty at institutions where student ratings are the only measure of teaching quality taken into account for retention, promotion, and tenure decisions, this carries a real threat. Not only does an institution lose its ability to accurately certify a student's skills, but the public will suffer from professionals who aren't really prepared to do their jobs.

Critics might argue that if a student isn't prepared, that is her problem. But what if that student has never mastered one particular aspect of computer programming and was able to pressure her instructor into changing her grade? After graduation she begins working for an aeronautics company designing a software program that will control key functions on a new airplane. There is a section of code that relies on the programming skills she didn't learn. As one of Georgia Tech's computer programming instructors, Bill Leahy, likes to ask students, "What if that plane is carrying puppies, your grandmother, and the cure for cancer?"

Students who pressure instructors for exceptional treatment are already common, so allowing them to consider themselves as "customers who are always right" only makes things worse. When I was a graduate student, a student came by my office just after spring term ended. He had received a grade of B plus in my freshman composition class, a grade that already reflected his taking advantage of some extra credit opportunities. His father had promised him a new car if he made a certain overall grade point average in his first year. I am fairly confident mine wasn't the lowest grade he had received, but there he was standing in my office asking for a grade change. When I said no, he pulled out his checkbook and asked how much it would take for me to change the grade. I answered, "If you had that kind of money you wouldn't need your daddy to buy you a car." He was angry, and retorted, "I provide your paycheck, and I can get you fired!" Having already been inspired to deliver one witty comeback, I was dumbstruck, and years later I would still be waiting for *l'esprit de l'escalier* if a colleague who had a similar encounter with a disgruntled student had not provided it the following term.

On that occasion, I was in the office of several graduate student colleagues, one of whom was the instructor of record for another freshman composition course. He entered the office, closely tailed by an angry student. They faced off, a desk between them. The student yelled, "My dad is a prominent attorney. If you don't change my grade, I am going to sue you for all you're worth!" My colleague, who had been civil for as long as possible, had had enough. He reached into his pocket, pulled out a stack of coins, slapped them down on the desk, and proclaimed in a stern but calm voice, "There you go. Now get the fuck out of my office." I have never been sure what surprised that student more, the fact that a graduate teaching assistant had dared to face off with him or the realization that the instructor had so little to lose.

Bribery and threats of litigation or worse are infrequent, but all professors have had experiences of students wheedling, or even demanding a different grade from the one that they earned. The more students *hear* that they are our customers, the more likely they will feel entitled to demand the grades they want—and instructors who fear losing their jobs will feel that pressure.

Academic integrity is another victim of the "customer is always right" mentality. Technology has enabled students to buy completed assignments online. A friend sent me a link to site that sells essays. The clear implication is that students may download these essays and pass them off as their own work. Paradoxically, the linked essay compares my MOOC articles to those written by Thomas Friedman.[9] While I find this amusing on the one hand, it also reminds me of some my most difficult student conferences.

Having the "you cheated" conversation with a student is never easy, but it can be particularly difficult if the student takes the "I'm the customer" stance. I have had students tell me it isn't plagiarism if they buy a paper because they paid for the right to use that material. This is not limited to students just out of high school, trying to flourish away from their parents from the first time. One of the most blatant cases I have heard of was described to me by a colleague who was serving on her university's Student Integrity Committee—the committee responsible for adjudicating cases of academic dishonesty. The accused student was enrolled in an executive MBA program. When confronted with the evidence that his paper had been copied from a website, he responded that he couldn't be held responsible because his secretary had copied and pasted the work. When the committee explained that having his secretary write the paper made the situation even worse, he coolly reminded them that he had paid handsomely for the exclusive program and that he expected them to back off—he had already purchased his diploma. He did have to submit another paper, but he graduated on time. Stories like these will only multiply if we allow students to think of themselves as retail customers.

A consumer viewpoint necessarily also implies a shorter-term perspective than a viewpoint in which the student is regarded as a learner and a moral agent undergoing personal growth. It is tempting for institutions to emphasize the salaries that their graduates are likely to earn upon graduation and to use this wealth creation as a measure of academic success. Some colleges have no choice. Starting salary is a factor used in the competitive ranking system for business schools, and this sets up a perverse incentive to send as many of their graduates as possible to parasitic financial positions (hedge fund managers, for example), rather than wealth-creating leadership positions in productive businesses, or lower-earning positions in government or not-for-profit organizations.

My institution, Georgia Tech, has been fortunate—it often ranks at the top of best values for colleges because its return on investment is excellent. (That is, the difference between increased lifetime earnings attributable to a Georgia Tech degree and the cost of that degree and its loan repayments is positive.) Georgia Tech ranks first for annual return on investment at 12 percent, and eighth for twenty-year net return on investment at $796,300.[10] Clearly this is a decision criterion for students (and their parents) when selecting a college. However, often when educational choices and priorities are discussed in terms of return on investment and preparation for the workforce, the true "customer" is not the student, but the sponsoring state and corporate constituents.

Students Do Not Always Want
What We Think They Want

When students represent such a large, heterogeneous proportion of the population, it's impossible to generalize about who "they" are or what they might need or want from an educational experience. MOOC students, in particular, have confounded proponents' expectations about who would flock to MOOCs and benefit most from them.

As an illustration of how dangerous it can be to generalize about students, consider DeMillo's assertion that universities must recognize a new population of international students who are very different and will, he predicts, want a very different kind of educational experience: "As each new billion joins free market economies and open societies, the definition of education is repeatedly jolted because the newcomers have different notions of what is valuable."[11] Logically speaking, DeMillo is absolutely correct to assume people from different cultures might expect different things from an educational experience than American students expect. However, these differences may run counter to expectations. When we have a strong agenda, the data can be disconcertingly recalcitrant.

For example, in 2014 Georgia Tech launched an online master's degree program in computer science (the "OMS"). This is a partner project with one of the original MOOC providers, Udacity, and has received a generous start-up investment from AT&T. The admissions demographics for the first cohorts of students were surprising to some people involved in the planning of that program.

Graduate programs are attractive to international students, so much so that many graduate programs rely on international students for their continuing viability. Fully 50 percent of Georgia Tech's graduate students come to the United States on student visas, the majority from China, India, and South Korea. Even more international students were expected to enroll in the OMS, possibly from less-served and economically disadvantaged nations. With a price tag of about $7,000, the OMS is affordable to all but those living in poverty and almost guarantees a rapid return on investment in the job market. However, the ratio of international to domestic students in the OMS was far lower than in the residential student population. For the 2015–16 academic year, it has expanded to 21 percent (the corresponding on-campus program is made up of 67 percent international students). Informal polls revealed what should have been obvious in advance: many degree-seeking international students want a degree as a passport to a job in the United States. A distance education course, however cheap, is of little more use to them than a residential degree from an institution in their home country. Having worked closely with graduate students for many years, I am aware that many of them enroll in American universities as a means of relocating here. Many of them never wish to return their home countries, and a student visa is an easy avenue for getting here, although not an inexpensive one.

Computer science programs nationwide also have difficulty attracting women into the field. The ratio of men to women in the College of Computing master's programs on campus at Georgia Tech is 2.6 to 1, which is low, but tracks national trends. An online degree, it was thought, would be more attractive to midcareer women who wanted to retool their professional skills, having perhaps temporarily dropped out of the job market to raise a family, or who lacked the option of relocating to a campus. Enrollment in the OMS has a ratio of men to women of 6.4 to 1. We had shifted the needle, but in the wrong direction. Here too, the data had trumped exhortations.

OMS designers also expected many students to take advantage of employers' programs to pay their tuition, but the OMS tuition is set so low that not all do this. Students would rather incur the cost personally so that they are not obliged—morally or legally—to report progress to or remain with their employer once they graduate.

Finally, the OMS was expected to appeal to students with first degrees from the best universities. Rigorous application standards are adhered to, and the most common bachelor's degree for OMS students is a Georgia Tech degree, not surprising given the loyalty that alumni feel toward their alma mater and the buzz that had surrounded the launch of the degree. Another common source for our initial group of admitted students came as a surprise, however: it was University of Phoenix graduates. Thus the attraction of a high-quality online degree appeals disproportionately to those who have experienced one already. Online universities deserve the criticisms they receive about low retention and six-year graduation rates. (The University of Phoenix has a six-year graduation rate for its four-year degrees of only 16 percent,[12] compared with Georgia Tech's 2015 rate of 85 percent.[13]) Nevertheless, when students do graduate, they are more likely to enroll in similar online programs like the OMS.

Managing Diversity

In our Composition 2.0 MOOC we appreciated the geographic diversity of our students every day. On one of the course's most prominent landing pages we had embedded a Google Map on which students could pin their locations. Beforehand we had prepared for the international and multicultural experience and spent much time discussing the expectations of students from other cultures. However, some came from places and backgrounds about which we had little knowledge.

For example, during one of our Google Hangout discussions, we reviewed key points about a reading assignment, a text by Martin Luther King, Jr. We quickly realized that a Turkish student had merely heard of King and did not understand enough about his life to place the reading in context. Knowing nothing about modern Turkish history, I tried to draw parallels between King and Gandhi, about whom I hoped the student would know. On another occasion, we assigned an audio recording of an essay by David Sedaris. While planning Composition 2.0, we discussed in depth whether to use this recording because Sedaris is generous in his use of profanity. With students from all over the world, we expected some to take offense. Eventually, we concluded that the recording met our learning objectives better than the alternatives, and we went ahead with it. During the MOOC we were surprised that there were no objections about the profanity, but we were equally taken aback by some confusion that the recording engendered. Even though we required a functional use of English as a course prerequisite, we had not predicted just how highly idiomatic was Sedaris's use of humor. In retrospect, we realize that we should have considered providing a listening guide to explain how Sedaris's style and language choices function.

We also misgauged our students' understanding of some technical or business and discipline-specific terms. At the outset of the course, we asked students to complete a "Personal Benchmark Statement." We assumed that college-level students who were fluent in English would understand the term "benchmark." We were wrong and added a glossary of terms to our site.

My experience as a woman presenting a MOOC, including the ways in which I felt emotionally exposed and threatened, as well as other, less negative experiences, grew out of the multicultural nature of a MOOC's student population, like a lengthy discussion surrounding my on-camera wardrobe and whether my choices were supposed to look "Indian" (see Chapter 7 for more details on this and other issues relating to gender). Perhaps the student who complained had been thinking along the same lines as I was doing about the Martin Luther King and Sedaris incidents. I wondered whether he thought I was trying too hard to relate to my non-Anglo students. I didn't feel threatened or demeaned by his comments, merely a bit perplexed and chastened that here was something else that I had misjudged, despite my best attempts.

Multicultural bridging conversations are not unknown in the classroom. Nine percent of our undergraduates and about half our graduate students at Georgia Tech are international students, and everyone on campus benefits from the diversity of cultural backgrounds. Moreover, we attract undergraduate students from every state in the union, from urban, suburban, and rural schools, and from a wide spectrum of ethnic and class backgrounds. So articulating shared assumptions is nothing new to the average college professor. Nevertheless, massive scaled education necessarily introduces more cultural misunderstandings and lessens the opportunity to deal with them. My team and our Turkish student were lucky that our misplaced assumptions about his knowledge surfaced during that hangout discussion. I am confident that many similar misunderstandings passed by unnoticed and untreated.

These examples illustrate a shortcoming on our part. Perhaps we could have been even more inclusive, aware, and culturally sensitive than we set out to be. There is always room for improvement. My conclusion, though, is that some residual lack of shared context is the inevitable background of any attempts at global online education—as long as the world remains culturally heterogeneous, that is. Totally eradicating misunderstandings such as the ones we had to deal with would only become a realistic goal if we assume a hegemonic canon of knowledge, and that would be a terrible price to pay for shared understanding. If Silicon Valley had grown up around the Dardanelles fifty years ago and today's Coursera were a Turkish company, I imagine that someone like me in that alternative universe would now be explaining to American students who Atatürk was.

Wherever they were from, our MOOC students (and students in all MOOCs) were not the underserved for whom MOOCs were intended or whose elevation from disadvantage and poverty the pro-MOOC rhetoric promised. In a 2013 survey of the 34,779 students who had enrolled in one of the University of Pennsylvania's MOOCs, researchers found 83 percent of students had a two- or four-year college degree. Furthermore, 44.2 percent had even completed some graduate education.[14]

We know that some students who knew the subject matter as well as we did were enrolled in Composition 2.0. Some self-identified writing and communication instructors were our students, not to brush up their knowledge and skills, of course, but to consider alternative ways to teach the subject and cheer us on (or, we suspected, like some NASCAR fans, watching in anticipation of accidents). These instructors even formed their own forum to share ideas about how they could use our course to teach their students. We reciprocated. Several Composition 2.0 team members enrolled as "embedded" students in a variety of MOOCs on different subjects offered at universities worldwide. Our goal was to better understand the student experience as well as how other instructors were using the MOOC format. These experiences made us rethink the how long our course was and how we clarified our expectations to our students. Very few faculty members attend each other's on-campus courses to garner ideas about how to teach more effectively. In MOOCs, this is quite common, and a small but vocal subpopulation of students is likely to be other academics.

Dial-Up Deprivation

It may seem obvious, but it requires stating: online education serves only students who are online. Even in the United States, many students who otherwise could benefit from a MOOC education have difficulty getting online service good enough to download or view the materials adequately. Going to the public library for a session on a five-year-old PC with child protection filters installed does not count. Students need to own their own computers, live where broadband is available, be able to afford the cost of broadband service or have convenient and reliable free Wi-Fi connections, and have the freedom in their daily lives to be online when they want and need to be. These requirements are not met by everyone's circumstances. Most people have to pay for Internet access at home, and in some countries access is too expensive for low-income citizens—the very citizens who might actually want basic job training.

As the Pew Research Center's Internet & American Life Project shows, only 70 percent of American adults had broadband Internet access from their homes in May 2013, but these percentages depend critically on socio-economic status:

> The demographic factors most correlated with home broadband adoption continue to be educational attainment, age, and household income. Almost nine in ten college graduates have high-speed Internet at home, compared with just 37 percent of adults who have not completed high school. Similarly, adults under age fifty are more likely than older adults to have broadband at home, and those living in households earning at least $50,000 per year are more likely to have home broadband than those at lower income levels.[15]

So access in the United States is as much about socioeconomics as anything else. Lower-income families, the least likely to attend college, are also those least likely to have broadband connections in the home, and therefore the least likely to study online. People who have already attended college and who make over $50,000 a year (the sector of the population who need MOOCs the least) are the ones who will have broadband. It is no surprise that so many of those who enroll in MOOCs already have a college degree.

Let me be clear. I agree we should be offering alternative ways for people to pursue college degrees or other educational opportunities. For me as a non-traditional student, community college was the answer. Using technology to reach people in rural areas (if we can provide broadband access) is important because some of these people may not be physically able to get to a campus of any kind. Veterans who suffer from combat-related post-traumatic stress are another group that might find online education a better fit for their needs.

Even if people have access to online courses, they may not possess the important technological literacies to be successful. Precisely because technological innovations have displaced them from the workforce, we have a population of middle-aged people who lack important skills to be successful in an online environment. Asking them to participate in new educational opportunities via technology that they don't understand or don't have access to is a cruel way to discourage them from exploring opportunities.

Never Mind the Quality, Feel the Width

Lowering the costs of any service is in the interest of customers, but lowering quality generally is not, unless there is a substantial trade-off in cost savings. Our priorities should therefore address this trade-off. Meaningful engagement with faculty is a critical determinant of student success, whether you are educating philosophers or welders.

We were able to mimic interactivity with students in Composition 2.0 by holding live-stream Google Hangout sessions with selected students that the rest of the enrolled students could watch. But for most of them, this was a passive experience of interaction by proxy. It is possible in smaller online settings to have good interaction between faculty and students, although this is usually different in character from face-to-face interaction. But at MOOC scale there is no meaningful way to engage the vast majority of students on a personal level. In my on-campus classes, which are typically small, I make it a personal mission to be actively involved with my students' learning and to know them as individuals. The absence of such interaction in the MOOC context was therefore jarring to me. The experience lacked something that gives personal meaning to the vocation of teaching, and I believe that most of the students did not experience the value of my teaching in the way that my traditional classroom experience makes commonplace.

Cost is often taken as a substitute for quality, to such an extent in the arena of higher education that many colleges want to appear more expensive than they really are. Like car dealerships offering "cash back" offers, exclusive private colleges and universities offer average "discount rates" of up to 50 percent, a financially unsustainable model in which they cite costs to prospective students and parents and then offer scholarships that reduce that cost by about half. You get what you pay for, as the saying goes. If these colleges were simply to cut their tuition, most applicants would go elsewhere for more expensive educations that must, perforce, be of higher quality.

Indeed, quality of outcomes is not only a moral imperative for universities; it is also healthy self-interest, and no punditry is needed to point this out. Graduating our students with the knowledge and skills that will make them successful, and by extension make the companies or organizations they work for more successful, is a goal that should never change. In fact, often their success becomes our success from a marketing standpoint, as universities are quick to say who our most successful graduates are, and because many graduates, highly successful or not, often become donors who give money to their alma maters out of a sense of shared pride and community allegiance.

This dynamic isn't the exclusive purview of elite schools. Many graduates of smaller schools are fiercely loyal to their schools. Even if they are unable to become donors, they are able to promote their school by talking about their own experience, and even in the case of a community college that doesn't have a national reputation, graduates may be extremely grateful for the opportunity that college provided for them. I am always quick to say how much my experiences in community college meant for my success. Since 2013, I have been honored to be named the Distinguished Alumna and to be featured in both an alumni magazine article and a promotional video for Georgia Perimeter College promoting the value of the associate's degree, a two-year degree often denigrated as "high school plus." Mine, though, is the one degree among the four I have earned of which I am the proudest, and which was the most difficult to obtain. Despite recommendations from colleagues who had more orthodox educations that I should expunge it from my vita, I talk about it proudly.[16] Much of my goodwill is the result of the interactions I had with my professors.

For Our Students' Sake

In a traditional classroom, I get to know the strengths and limitations of all the students in my classes. This knowledge lets me adapt lesson plans to their needs on the fly. Small-scale distance learning courses need not lack this capability for adaptation, because ample engagement mechanisms exist, such as forums, chats, videoconferences, emails, and even occasional in-person meetings. MOOCs do not have this flexibility. A prerecorded presentation and threaded discussion forums with tens of thousands of participants talking across each other mean that the needs of the student who could benefit from extra engagement or some accommodation are ignored. Even when students make suggestions about the course (as ours did), their feedback cannot be acted on until the next offering of the course. The professional media production facilities needed for a successful MOOC mean that materials have to be "in the can" well before they are released.

In the face of these production realities, the idealism and exhortations of pundits ring hollow:

> Daphne Koller, a Stanford computer science professor who is one of the founders of Coursera, which offers free online courses from sixty-two colleges and universities, stressed the importance of online education for students' sake. "It's important to maintain academic freedom, but it's important for faculty to understand the constraints that students are living under," she said. Her company was founded primarily to serve students who were not enrolled on a traditional campus, and she acknowledged that online education was not right for all students.[17]

I'm familiar with the constraints that students live under from my own experiences and from being sensitive to what my students do and say. A few years ago, I had a graduate student in my dissertation writing class. His entire village had saved money for years to send him to college. Failure of any kind was not an option. He felt the weight of his burden every day, and he worried that he might not be able to graduate. One afternoon, after a difficult meeting with his advisor, he came to me in tears. He was distraught. I walked with him to our counseling center because I was deeply concerned he might try to harm himself. I breathed a huge sigh of relief the day he successfully defended his dissertation. Acknowledging the investments (financial and otherwise) that students (and their family and friends) make in their education is an essential part of being a responsible member of the academic community. No matter who our students are, or where they are from, we must respect their investment in their own educational process. Therefore, our primary responsibility should be to our students, not their future employers.

We must be willing to ask ourselves what we want higher education to mean for everyone, rather than for an elite few. If we decide we want that education to represent a finite set of skills that prioritize various companies' needs, then the answer will be a system that favors vocational training over broader learning. If, however, we decide we want higher education to represent a broad set of skills that prioritize an individual student's development over a lifetime, which could include a variety of jobs, then philosophy, as one example, will be as valuable to a welder as it is to a corporate executive.

SIX

Only the *Countable* Counts

American students are conditioned from their earliest educational experiences to think about what *counts* when attempting to assess what is being asked of them: How many points is this question worth? Will there be any extra credit on the exam? How much will this assignment count toward the final course grade? Will the grades be curved? Will I ever use this in the future? Why do I have to take a course outside my major? With our focus on the most immediate and easiest-to-understand measures, it should be no surprise that as a culture we seek to quantify the educational experience as a whole.

Weights and Measures

Standardization and testing practices have been common practice in K-12 education for at least thirty years, culminating in the 2000s in No Child Left Behind. What these tests often determine, of course, is whether a student is a good test taker, not whether he or she has mastered the skills being tested. The perpetuation of such procedures depends on nonacademic incentives, such as the ranking or funding of the institution from which the student has come or to which he or she is hoping to go. No Child Left Behind has generated immense controversy because schools and teachers are rewarded and penalized for the educational preparedness of their students, not the effects of their teaching. In 2015, eleven Atlanta public school teachers and officials were convicted of racketeering for inflation of student scores on standardized tests. The prosecution alleged that the director of the school system had threatened to fire principals and teachers whose students' test scores did not increase, and a pervasive conspiracy to falsify results ensued.

The College Board's SAT (Scholastic Aptitude Test) predicts a test taker's family wealth better than college success,[1] and as a consequence many US colleges and universities have adopted "test optional" admissions policies. Very few, however, have gone "test blind" (meaning that the institution refuses to consider standardized test scores when making admission decisions), because an average SAT, or converted ACT (American College Testing), score is used by *US News and World Report* in generating its college and university rankings. Sarah Lawrence College, one of the most prestigious liberal arts schools in the United States, was test blind from 2005 until 2013, but toward the end of that period its administration decided that the school's reputation was suffering because test blindness was disqualifying it from rankings. The intermediate "test optional" position, which neither requires nor ignores standardized test results, allows colleges and universities to be ranked without forcing them to take test results into account in admissions. This can let private institutions incorporate factors that improve the diversity of the student body, although there is no evidence that this has happened.[2] A less noble motivation is that an institution's ranking is likely to be inflated by this policy: students with the highest scores have an incentive to submit them, knowing that this will benefit their chances, while those with lower scores have an incentive not to submit them, thereby inflating the average scores that the institution can claim.

High-stakes tests, like the SATs or end-of-semester final exams, are summative assessments because they sum up the student's achievements in a single measure. By the time the grade is reported, it is too late for the student to make direct use of any feedback. However, other assessment-like events (low-stakes tests, practice quizzes, etc.) can occur much earlier for formative assessment. This type of assessment tells the student something of value about how he or she is learning and preparing. When students have narrow communication with instructors and assistants, as happens in a MOOC because of the large number of students potentially asking for help, efficient formative assessment methods are particularly important. During Composition 2.0, we put much effort into designing formative and rapid assessment techniques, but we were thwarted by platform design and the unwillingness of the support team to understand the educational requirements we were bringing to them.

For example, we placed quizzes for self-assessment in the middle of videos. A student watched some of the video, answered a question, watched some more, answered another question, and so on. Many of our students complained because they were not able to complete in-video quizzes when they downloaded the lecture videos and were thus denied the engagement and pedagogically valuable feedback. Perhaps in Silicon Valley all homes have adequate bandwidth for local students to live-stream videos without artifacts and lag effects, but many of our students were not so fortunate. To improve their viewing experience, some students needed to download videos to watch later. Our instructional team wanted to help students with limited Internet access complete their work off-line. We could not provide a way to do so, and so we pressed the Coursera support staff for a solution, but they could not provide one. Although it was convenient to embed the questions in the high-bandwidth video, and engaging for the students who had access to streaming media, the video and questions could have been easily decoupled. The downloads and quizzes could instead have been served from a common contents page.

Worse still, in some MOOC courses, but not ours, performance on these formative assessments counts toward a personal score that determines whether a student can be recognized as completing the course. Students with inadequate connections therefore cannot feasibly pass such courses. It's shocking that scenarios like this did not arise during the design of their platform (or were disregarded when they did arise), given that reaching developing nations and underserved students in rural areas is one of the often-quoted benefits of MOOCs.

When such difficulties occurred, the design of the platform and the marketing of the course by Coursera conspired to place me inadvertently in an awkward situation. I felt that I needed to send an announcement by email to all the enrolled students to explain why we could not address a problem they had brought to our attention. Most students were flexible and responded with understanding. They appreciated our effort to communicate transparently. However, we did not want to apologize for the shortcomings of our technology or say anything that distanced ourselves from the quality of the students' experience. It was easy to understand why students become frustrated when using a remote and impersonal platform.

What is going on here is that development staff who lack the necessary perspective are making significant decisions that embed assumptions about the nature of successful teaching and learning. It's not their fault; they're not bad people. It's even possible that some of these changes, if they had been anticipated, could have been introduced from the start without incurring extra development costs; so it is not necessarily the case that Coursera's business imperatives detracted from our educational goals. It is simply that software platforms force educational choices on their professional users that no one from the development team with the required competence and training has vetted. There were other examples.

For one, we were originally set to begin the MOOC in early April 2013. We delayed the start by over a month because of technical problems and misunderstandings about procedures. Some of the issues were related to our pedagogical choices, but others were a result of our unfamiliarity with the platform. We also faced an administrative challenge because C21U, the unit at Georgia Tech overseeing all the MOOCs, did not want our team talking directly to Coursera—rather they asked that we funnel questions through their office, which often resulted in delays while we waited for answers. Eventually, C21U arranged for the reassignment of an IT specialist to consult with us about the platform and speed up the time it took for us to get answers to our questions and respond to our requests.

Through our IT specialist, we learned that we needed to extend our timeline and change curricular features we thought were necessary for adequate learning. For example, we wanted to have students review the short writing samples they would produce while taking quizzes during sessions of the course, but we discovered that students' answers would not be available to them after they submitted their quiz—stored, yes, but not available."[3] This was another shocking shortcoming that flies in the face of standard teaching practice for writing courses.

Perhaps these are all early problems with MOOC platforms that will be of little interest in a few years, as the technology develops and the platform companies that emerge and survive listen to educators. Such accidents of history are frustrating but ephemeral. However, in the case of a course like ours, there are more essential features of the assessment process—whether formative or summative—when a student is learning to write. All subject matter tests are vulnerable to overemphasis on what can most easily be tested, and all teaching can be perverted into "teaching to the test," but it is process-based skills like writing that are the most likely to be assessed poorly because standardized tests usually use objective-based methods.

Illusory Objectivity and the Challenge of Scale

A danger with all testing is that educators are interested in many levels of a student's understanding (see Bloom's Taxonomy).[4] Unfortunately, devising and scoring test items at the low levels of learning sophistication, which is what we should be least interested in assessing, are far simpler to do with easily administered multiple-choice questions than is assessing more sophisticated learning outcomes. In my experience, creative skills, such as technical or creative writing or design, cannot be assessed this way. What needs to be mastered and assessed in these areas are *process* skills, not the quality of the *products* produced, which are a poor sampling indicator of skills. This makes attempts to fragment and quantify learning in these subject matter areas impossible.

Many STEM skills are less open to interpretation than are writing and communication ability, and are therefore easier to assess. The economic emphasis on STEM education conveniently focuses attention on the very topics that are most amenable to standardized teaching and assessment. There are right answers and wrong answers. But where my colleagues in the sciences can rely on the online administration of multiple-choice tests and machine grading, assessing a student essay requires that a qualified human actually read it.

This is not to say that higher-level learning of STEM knowledge and skills amounts to learning the right answers to simple multiple-choice questions. To become a scientist or an engineer requires mastery of skills in the context of experiments, research papers, and formal lab reports, and these competencies are just as difficult to assess using simple machine grading. However, there is a crucial difference in emphasis. In a STEM course, much of the content can be delivered by online courses and learning can be assessed mechanistically. Those parts that cannot can then be the topic of face-to-face interactions in the classroom. Indeed, it is this insight that has led to the use of MOOC course materials in "flipped" or "blended" courses. In composition courses, by contrast, writing is not just an isolated assignment. It is *the* foundational component. So how does one assess a student's progress? Assessment of writing is nowhere near as amenable to machine grading as STEM knowledge. It is nuanced, time-consuming, and difficult.

For all these reasons, composition classes tend to be smaller than classes in the STEM disciplines. Providing formative and summative feedback about student writing is labor-intensive, textually rich, contextualized, and time-consuming. The Conference on College Composition and Communication (CCCC), which is a subset of the National Council of Teachers of English (NCTE), has for many years issued position statements related to the best practices in teaching college writing. CCCC's most recent policy statement on class size recommends that sections should ideally enroll only fifteen students, with twenty students being the absolute maximum.[5] In the first two college composition classes at Georgia Tech, our class sizes are higher than this, at twenty-five—a number many of our colleagues from other disciplines, especially in STEM disciplines, believe should be even larger. Contrast this with science teaching. At Georgia Tech, the allowable enrollment for our freshman physics class is 192, a number that I believe is far too high (at least without highly qualified teaching assistants) if these courses include any open-ended writing assignments. The strict adherence to the CCCC's recommendations is one reason some of my disciplinary colleagues opposed experiments in massive courses. Any attempt to teach composition at scale was, they believed, inherently a betrayal of what it means to be a composition teacher.

CCCC is far from being a Luddite organization. As I explained in Chapter 2, writing centers and composition teachers were among the earliest innovators in technology-infused teaching. As a community of educators, we have embraced the importance of the relationship between writing and technology—perhaps having considered the pedagogical connections more than many other disciplines. Rarely today will you find a college composition course rubric that does not incorporate technology use as one of the evaluation factors. And CCCC's policies state that "sound writing instruction emphasizes relationships between writing and technologies."[6] However, composition instructors never work in the binary world of zeros and ones; we are always interested in nuance and subtlety. We recognize that a profound approach to evaluation and feedback is necessary.

At the time I was teaching Composition 2.0, there were three other composition-focused MOOCs funded by the same Gates Foundation grant program that funded ours: San Jacinto Community College, Duke University, and Ohio State University. All of us faced criticism from disciplinary peers who assumed we were "traitors" even to flirt with distance learning at scale in a subject where intense student-faculty interaction is a hallmark. We wanted, so the criticism goes, to undermine what quality writing instruction is. It's a "slippery slope" argument: once we open the door a crack, newer technology-driven changes will flood in, diluting what was once an engaged learning experience and leading to shallow learning and poor writing by our students.

Bits and Pieces of Learning

The move away from integrative learning toward a fragmented, quantified, and instrumental approach to schooling was well under way when I was in high school in the early 1980s. We were required to take competency tests to prove we had certain basic skills, but it wasn't until my return to academic life after a hiatus of ten years that I realized how far the obsession with test results had gone. The Advanced Placement (AP) exams were only just taking off for college-bound students when I went to high school. Many, although certainly not all, of my friends and I sat the PSAT and the SAT, although I cannot remember any of us actually studying for the tests. We didn't even talk about tests except in the days just before one was administered—and then mostly we only complained about having to give up a Saturday morning for that purpose.

The newer AP courses and exams can exempt a student from some otherwise required courses in college. To measure and rank students on a standardized scale, academics have to agree to fragment their profession into distinct disciplines and then fragment those disciplines into readily compared and fungible subjects and courses. In the University System of Georgia, for example, each institution participates in a system of transferable general education courses. With common naming and numbering, credit for such courses automatically transfers when a student moves from one institution to another. There is no need in these cases for a student to justify to a faculty member or administrator that the course credit he or she is coming in with is of the required standard for the new institution. Similarly, high school subjects and AP classes have agreed upon scope and depth, so that students from different high schools can be compared fairly. These transfer systems rely on instructors and administrators at all levels not making local decisions about what counts in a subject. If one university declared that introductory calculus should contain some integration and another decided that it did not, the benefits of standardized fragmentation would be lost. No one teaching a follow-on course would know whether students were adequately prepared or, conversely, whether some of the more "advanced" material duplicated what students had already been taught.

Fragmentation and standardization are therefore crucial elements of higher education and its inflowing high school pipeline. Once subjects are distinguished and subdivided along common fracture lines, it then becomes feasible to compare them. Which are the most economically productive? Which are the most popular? Again, there are feasible measurements that encourage comparisons and rankings, and less feasibly measured values that become suppressed in our discourse. This is the root of the ongoing devaluation of the arts and humanities.

One way to explicitly measure and promote the exogenous value of subjects is by the introduction of credentials below the level of the degree. Instead of majors, we have a menagerie of minors, certificates, microcredentials, and "badges" (the latter deriving their names from the Boy and Girl Scouts' method for assigning wearable credit for specific competencies). As a consequence of the logic of this certificate model, Christiansen and Eyring, among others, advocate that universities become more narrowly focused in the subject matter they offer. Like for-profit providers, universities should consider "the subjects in greatest demand."[7] One is left to wonder about students who are interested in subjects that have limited demand. The freedom to make meaningful decisions about pursuing one's vocation could be squashed in the process of cutting courses. While these authors recommend culling with care, they are nevertheless keen to encourage a wholesale reduction in advanced, specialized courses that meet a low demand and the introduction of a logically modularized approach to curricula.

So the identification of modules, courses, majors, and other nuggets of learning large and small is an essential component of the valuation of education. One cannot evaluate what one cannot measure, and one cannot measure what one cannot individuate. It is this tendency to subdivide that permits us to talk about "stackable credentials" and "competencies" that can be disaggregated from a holistic vision of learning and reaggregated into a series of achievements that could potentially count for a degree. Not surprisingly, the alternative providers, such as the MOOC platforms, are rooted in a model of knowledge whose fragmentation and measurement are unproblematic and noncontroversial. When dealing with subject matter that is infused with interpretation and perspectival thinking, such as learning to write, these writers and developers are nonplussed: according to them, measurement is measurement; content is content; and learning is skill acquisition.

Perhaps this is why the programmers at Coursera could not understand the problem with passing students through the peer-review training module after seven attempts—even if a student did not successfully master the training and was therefore not demonstrably able to critique fellow students' work. Since our course was predicated on peer review for evaluation, it was necessary that the evaluators (the students themselves) have the same skills. Though we explained the importance of the training module, we could not get a change that would prevent students from engaging in peer review if they did not pass the module. Even students in the course complained, as well they should have, but to no avail. Peer review is the only feasible assessment method in a MOOC if machine grading is impossible (as it was in our case.) We were surprised it had not been anticipated. If a platform provider is unwilling to address something this fundamental, then granting credit on the basis of completion and easily finessed quizzes is extremely problematic.

Machine Grading of Writing

In STEM disciplines a student can demonstrate learning (even sophisticated learning) by correctly calculating a value by the appropriate application of a formula to some disguised but critical aspect of a technical problem. Once the question has been set, hundreds of students can be assessed and their grades assigned instantaneously by machine comparisons of their answers against a correct value. Writing instructors have resisted this approach to assessing writing for at least two reasons. First, there is no common "formula" for deriving the "right" answer to a writing prompt. The most one can do is to articulate a formal rubric of the kinds of attributes that good writing displays and acceptable levels of these attributes.

But there is a second and more obvious difficulty with machine grading of writing. It can't be done. How can someone program a computer to check whether a complex thesis statement is complete and supportable? How can it assess whether the appropriate disciplinary style been achieved in a piece of writing? How can it evaluate whether the evidence presented is valid for the thesis at hand? The problem is that algorithms cannot yet substitute for human evaluation where higher-order concerns are in question. You can use some weak proxies, such as counting the number of times connective words like "because" and "therefore" appear, compute the average sentence length as an index of sophisticated thought, or compare the words used against an online lexicon to assess the writer's vocabulary. To satisfy the short-answer algorithm we used for our MOOC, a student could, practically speaking, answer "I Trout" and get credit. Why? In the case of this particular personal response we asked only that there be a pronoun and something else for the answer to be "complete." Granted we were not using the most complex of machine-grading technologies, but machines all suffer from a flaw: they are only as flexible and as smart as the person who programmed them.

During a public meeting at Georgia Tech in 2013, I asked Coursera co-founder Daphne Koller if she thought her platform was appropriate for teaching a writing course. She answered that she was unsure whether writing style or complex skills could be taught on the platform, even though there were robo-grading programs capable of detecting mechanical errors in writing. More recently, I was introduced to Sebastian Thrun, founder of another MOOC platform, Udacity. When the dean of Georgia Tech's College of Computing, Zvi Galil, made the introduction, he told Thrun that I was the one who had taught a MOOC on writing. Without prompting, Thrun replied that at Udacity they had decided against such courses because they understood the challenges were too great.

Despite encouraging noises from some scholars,[8] current machine-grading algorithms are embarrassingly easy to defeat by writing carefully crafted nonsense. Les Perelman's research on machine grading has demonstrated for many years that machines can evaluate some basic grammatical and mechanical errors, but higher-order issues cannot be effectively evaluated.[9] He has written nonsense essays that score very high in machine-grading environments because the mechanical elements of the writing are good. The April 2013 NCTE Position Statement on Machine Scoring explains in detail why machine grading remains unviable for evaluating writing.[10]

Nevertheless, discussions about machine grading, especially for general education courses, are significant. The recurring arguments take an alarming form:

ARGUMENT FOR MACHINE GRADING (ABSTRACT VERSION)

Premise 1:   Machine grading is better than nothing.
Premise 2:   Anything that is better than nothing is worth using.
Conclusion: Machine grading is worth using.

Inside jokes that academics make among themselves (or worse, to students) that they grade papers by dropping them down stairs and seeing which ones fall the farthest, only serve to undermine our professional credibility and permit the fallacious equation of what we do with "nothing."

If it were not for economic and rhetorical pressures to scale up "delivery" of education—pressures that MOOCs relieve by abdicating responsibility to assess quality—such arguments would be easy to debunk as vacuous. But with these pressures, one can sympathize with administrators who buy into the rhetoric of effortless assessment. Where only elite schools have the luxury to teach writing in ways that provide them the most substantive feedback to students, a revised version of the vacuous general argument for machine grading starts to look more compelling:

ARGUMENT FOR MACHINE GRADING
(ECONOMIC EXIGENCY VERSION)

Premise 1:   Machine grading is better than nothing.
Premise 1a: Nothing is all that we can afford to provide.
Premise 1b: Machine grading is cheap.
Premise 2:   Anything cheap that is better than nothing is worth using.
Conclusion: Machine grading is worth using.

In my article, "Are MOOCs the Future of General Education?,"[11] I discuss machine grading at length, with a particular focus on what is possible where. One of the luxuries of a small, private (usually elite) school, is that the faculty can spend more time providing substantive feedback to every student. In a large, public community college, an instructor teaching five courses per term will struggle to provide anything more than the most critical feedback. Machine grading may be better than nothing, but my experience teaching in different kinds of institutions (a community college, a liberal arts college, and three public research universities—two of them in the elite Association of American Universities [AAU] tier) has shown me that most students get more feedback from their instructors than what a machine could foreseeably provide.

For disruption advocates, the technological possibility of a machine that could grade quickly and effectively must sound like a siren call. The cost savings for eliminating graders, teaching assistants, and instructors would definitely be significant. Perhaps this is one reason there seems to be a conflation between machine grading and MOOCs, even though machine grading exists outside MOOCs, and MOOCs could conceivably avoid machine grading (e.g., by separating all assessment into in-person proctored exams at regional locations). In my opinion, MOOCs preclude any possibility of substantive evaluation unless an army of evaluators is employed—offering substantive feedback for seventy-five students can be an overwhelming task, but offering similar evaluation for twenty-five thousand students is impossible.

An alternate mode of evaluation is peer assessment. Here students are trained to apply rubrics developed by the instructor, and in the process they learn the skills of critical reading and editing—skills they can then apply reflectively to their own writing. Composition instructors have used peer assessment in teaching writing for many years, and it has become established pedagogical practice. We tried this in Composition 2.0, but with nearly twenty-two thousand students, and because of the platform limitations described earlier, it was impossible to assure the quality of the feedback students were receiving from their peers.

Hence, where MOOCs are concerned, machine grading is an unavoidable necessity. MOOCs must have some form of machine grading for evaluation, precisely because they are massive. Consequently, we reach an impasse. If machine grading is not viable, then the platform providers must employ graders or testing centers to facilitate evaluation outside the MOOC platform, and it is difficult to see how this would scale. As Reeves argues, "regardless of the type of delivery system, assessment strategies must be carefully aligned with other components of the learning environment . . . and with the inherent technological affordances."[12] MOOCs magnify the issues connected with a lack of qualitative and substantive evaluation in courses that require writing and other assignments that require qualitative assessment, and while peer review may help provide some early feedback, expert evaluation remains indispensable.

During the first months of developing our MOOC, I reminisced about the popular children's toy Farmer Says, which was designed in the 1960s to help children learn the names and associated sounds of common animals.[13] I learned from my Farmer Says that pigs go "oink," but I realized how impoverished my appreciation of pigs was when, as an eight-year-old, I was taken by my parents to the South Carolina State Fair. Somewhere beyond my basic content knowledge there was a need for something more—something that required a more personalized and involved engagement with the beautiful porcine complexity of the real thing in the flesh. I cannot comment from personal experience on the value of machine grading in the STEM fields where quantitative assessment may be the most appropriate form of evaluation, but when it comes to writing, grammar and mechanics are nothing more than the equivalent of sounds made by a toy.

SEVEN

The Superstar Professor

MOOCs are teacher-centered approaches to education because everything is predicated on "delivery of content." Teaching becomes cinematic performance art. In my experience, there was little room for interaction with students or the fielding of questions in a meaningful, interactive, and ongoing way. Of course, there are tools on most MOOC platforms to facilitate interaction—there must be some mechanism for student-initiated communication for teaching to occur at all—but the volume of information transmission in the other direction dwarfs any such attempt at using interactive teaching methods. Like a microcosm of the post–net neutrality Internet, a MOOC is one-way traffic. Students download, downlink, and stream, whereas instructors provide content.

Thus, in online platforms, the pedagogue must play two roles: authority figure and presenter. As authority figure, he or she must communicate knowledge that is taken to be accurate and relevant. As presenter, he or she must convey enthusiasm and clarity. Throughout the history of education these two roles have been conflated in the classroom, but in the world of correspondence courses, distance education, and MOOCs, the authority figure can potentially be pushed behind the curtain as a mere scriptwriter, while the presenter moves to center stage. After providing the course content, the instructor could, arguably, be replaced by an actor on camera.

Such separation is still rare, however, and is restricted to highbrow popular culture, such as television documentaries, rather than distance education courses or MOOCs. Since 2005, Alan Alda, for example, has been the host of the Public Broadcasting Service's series *Scientific American Frontiers.* According to the show's website, "Alan's natural curiosity and his enthusiasm for science have made him the ideal host." Viewers are invited to join him "once again as he takes us from the depth of the conscious mind to the outer reaches of the universe," and to "Write to Alan," who "welcomes questions and comments from *Frontiers* viewers!"[1] Sadly, most viewers' questions do not "plumb the depths of the conscious mind," nor do they "explore the outer reaches of the universe." They include such softballs as, "What is the funniest part of doing the show?" and "What is your favorite animal?"[2]

To his credit, Alda is no mere reader of scripts. His interest in science is genuine—he founded the Alan Alda Center for Communicating Science, and its signature event, the Flame Challenge,[3] a contest for explaining complex scientific concepts to an audience of eleven-year-olds. Consequently, Alda's enthusiasm and passing knowledge can come across as authoritativeness. However, playing a M.A.S.H. doctor on screen for many years does not make him an MD—or a PhD. In fact, the online credits for *Scientific American Frontiers* reveal he neither writes, produces, nor directs the show. Moreover, the scientists and engineers he interviews are not credited. We live in a culture where celebrity is either taken to imply credibility or, in the absence of plausible credibility, draws the consumer into compliance. Movie actors like Gwyneth Paltrow often give life, fashion, home improvement, and health advice. If Jennifer Aniston drinks SmartWater, or if David Beckham shops at H&M, then so will millions of their fans—not because Aniston or Beckham are seen as authorities in any traditional sense, but merely because fans want to emulate them. And let's face it, Paltrow, Aniston, and Beckham look good—exactly the way superstars should.

Likewise, in descriptions of university teaching, the "superstar professor" becomes a mythic construct in which excellence in both roles (authority and presenter) is wrapped up in a single heroic personage. Richard Feynman, a superstar if ever there was one, wrote and gave a celebrated series of introductory lectures on physics that serve as a good example of someone at the pinnacle of a research field (particle physics, in his case) also being a legendary communicator of basic concepts to freshman college students. Feynman's 1977 three volumes were republished as a commemorative boxed set in 2011.[4]

Today an academic like Feynman can achieve superstardom only by virtue of a stellar research career. It is not enough to be supremely knowledgeable about others' contributions or to be a magnificent teacher. Those were medieval virtues, not modern ones. DeMillo traces the concept of the superstar scholar—though not that term, of course—back to the medieval monasteries that preceded the earliest universities. He introduces medieval scholars like Thomas Aquinas and Saint Anselm, along with his book's eponym, Peter Abelard, as being charismatic, and "popular [because they showed] followers how to use logical, systematic tools to reopen debates that had been considered settled."[5] Essentially, DeMillo is introducing a group of "superstar" lecturers. Here we have a group of men who gained fame as teachers—there were no extensive research labs then: "[Abelard's] real contribution to the West was the establishment of schools organized around his teachings and methods. He was famous for using rational argument to best the leading scholars of the day, but it was no doubt his arrogance, stature, and striking looks that also drew thousands of students from across the civilized world to his lectures."[6] Imperious stage presence, crackling intellect, a square jaw: these are the things of superstardom. Yet arrogance is an odd attribute for DeMillo to glorify. This seems more a reflection of a modern viewpoint, where superstar researchers often are arrogant, especially in the company of those who prioritize teaching over research. And then there is the comment about Abelard's physical appearance, a comment that diminishes Abelard as a pure intellect. Is DeMillo suggesting that Abelard would not have become a superstar if he had been unattractive? Of course, charisma originates from many sources, and being physically striking may suffice if attractiveness is lacking. Socrates was nothing if not charismatic, but he was also famously ugly.

Whatever the reasons, lecture-style teaching appeals to the ham actor in most professors, and where this mode of staged presentation is most central to pedagogy, the temptation merely to perform at the expense of meaningful teaching is the greatest. For historical reasons DeMillo documents in some detail, he makes Europe ground zero for teaching as performance: "European university courses are performance art. They are stages for the professors."[7] Again, he engages in a telling rhetorical move, similar to his earlier diminishment of Abelard as an attractive man. The turn of phrase here places readers in a space that trivializes university lectures and the professors who deliver them. They are, in fact, merely actors upon a stage. But worse, as writers, directors, and producers of their own productions, DeMillo reveals their vanity as they "strut" in front of their captive audience. If these "instructors" are merely pedantically extoling their own research, I grant a kind of acting—or at least, pontification. Perhaps it is different in Italy, but in Germany, where I have been a visiting scholar for twelve years, I have never seen an instructor strut in front of an audience; in fact, I suspect most of the students and instructors at the Technische Universität Dortmund would describe my guest lectures as the most theatrical they've seen.

For instructors who have already attained superstar status in their field, teaching a MOOC could be similar to the way they normally interact with students. If they design, write, and present lectures in their large and popular courses but have junior instructors or teaching assistants handle the grade assignments and interactions with students, then not much would be different following the migration of a course to a MOOC platform. Michael Sandel of Harvard University has taught a course on justice (accompanied by his best-selling book of the same name)[8] for about twenty years to many Harvard students, including one offering that was taken by over a thousand students. It was recorded in the classroom in 2005 and made freely available online, and subsequently redone with professional recording standards and released as a MOOC on the EdX platform. This is such a large course that it requires a supporting organization even when taught in the flesh.

But not everyone can be a superstar. When the winner takes all, there are lots of losers. And for every Hollywood superstar there are many would-be actors or screenplay writers driving cabs and waiting tables, hoping for the call that will never come. Superstardom when applied to teaching implies the same logic of scarcity—unless those in the academic chorus line resist.

Problems arise concerning the professional status of teachers when an institution acquires the rights to such a MOOC, thus relegating its own faculty to the status of Harvard teaching assistants. San Jose State University adopted Sandel's MOOC in 2013, and the faculty of its Philosophy Department soon refused to teach a course that used it and wrote an open letter to Sandel accusing him of complicity in the undercutting of their professional status.[9]

My observations of many colleagues who have considered teaching MOOCs (only some of whom decided to take the plunge) is that without question, some instructors become interested in teaching MOOCs primarily because they imagine a certain kind of fame will accompany the experience—an enticing proposition for those in a field rarely associated with celebrity. The possibility of fame is one reason some faculty are more interested in MOOCs than they have been in traditional distance education.

For more traditional distance education courses with much smaller numbers of students interacting on private platforms, exposure is limited. Many forms of media encourage innovators to brand themselves or to invest in the "start-up of you."[10] Therefore, it is no surprise that academics are as likely to seek fame as anyone else. For some who take the next step of committing, the possibility of fame makes the additional workload of designing, producing, and delivering a MOOC worth the time and effort, not to mention a compensation for the lack of proportional remuneration. It can be difficult not to fall prey to notions of vanity, and even I occasionally felt those pressures during the process of my MOOC.

Throughout my work about MOOCs, I have reflected on the issue of celebrity.[11] Hollywood representations of teachers are often grandiose depictions within the plot (think: Lulu singing "To Sir with Love," or the students atop desks bellowing, "O Captain, My Captain!" in *Dead Poets' Society*), but even films depict fame as arising not *from* teaching, but rather from a teacher's personal story and struggle. In fact, as viewers we tend to adopt sympathy for the underappreciated but noble teacher depicted on the screen. And so it can be with MOOCs. A certain kind of ephemeral fame is possible, but perhaps not what many people imagine. As I have explained elsewhere[12] and will elucidate later in this chapter, for me there were countervailing personal costs. Fame, like MOOCs, has a price.

Goodbye, Mr. Chips

In 2015, I was invited to a conference at Wageningen University in the Netherlands to give a presentation about MOOC course design and implementation. On the flight, I watched the 2014 movie *The Rewrite*, in which a character played by Hugh Grant is forced to take a teaching position at a small college because his career as a screenwriter has tanked. I generally avoid movies about teaching because they so distort the profession, and when the message is, "Those who can, do; those who cannot, teach," my antipathy is reinforced. But it was a long flight, and Hugh Grant is irresistible. In *The*

Rewrite, Grant's character was once a young, superstar screenwriter. Now in his early fifties, after years of steady decline, he can't find work; in desperation, he takes a job as a visiting writer in Binghamton, New York. After satisfying the Hollywood plot device of falling into bed with a young coed, and then beginning to fall in love with a nontraditional student, he slowly finds himself influencing his students' lives. He likes this. And despite his protestations early in the film that nothing important can be taught, he comes to learn some important lessons about himself. When he faces losing his job when his unprofessional sexual dalliances are revealed, he realizes how much his new job has come to mean to him. He makes an impassioned plea for a second chance, and (because this is a movie) he gets one. Along the way, he changes the lives of several students, including helping one young man get his screenplay accepted by a studio—allowing him a new legacy.

But how does a washed-up screenwriter become a competent creative writing teacher? Grant's character's answer is simple: go and watch *Dead Poets' Society.* This is an arch movie buff's inside joke, a clever piece of movie title product placement, and an homage to the late actor Robin Williams, all wrapped up in a package of meta-level ironies. However, taken at face value, the confused messages presented in this movie and many others should bother all educators.

First, the notion that anyone down on his or her luck can simply walk into a classroom and suddenly begin making colossal improvements in his or her students' academic and personal lives bespeaks an attitude in which teaching is regarded at best as a hereditary gift, and at worst as something anyone can do. There is no need, indeed no point, in learning how to do it well or preparing for a class. You may be a superstar teacher without realizing it—not, at least, until your unsuccessful experience in the "real world" propels you into the sanctuary of the ivy-clad classroom. The reality of teaching is that it takes much more to be successful than doing what Williams's character did in *Dead Poets' Society:* walking into the room and dramatically instructing students to tear out the introduction pages of their textbooks. And one rarely finds students who are so ready to transcend the entire college experience and go directly into a million-dollar dream job as the Grant character's student did. If this kind of Hollywood validation is what you want, teaching is not the career for you.

So why do movies like *The Rewrite*; *Dead Poets' Society*; *To Sir, with Love*; *Lean on Me*; *Dangerous Minds*; *Stand and Deliver*; *Mr. Holland's Opus*; *Goodbye, Mr. Chips*; *The Emperor's Club*; *Educating Rita*; and even *School of Rock*, appeal so strongly to moviegoers in the United States? Audiences love this kind of film, in which either the teacher or the students are down on their luck; it is even better if everyone is, because this reveals education as a redeeming factor. The teacher requires only dedication and natural, unschooled talent (though, possibly, as in the case of Mr. Chips, many years of slowly transformative experience) to be ready to change lives. It is a plot that functions as an analogue of the American dream.

Unrealistic depictions of teaching are culturally ingrained in the American mindset. Perhaps this is why so much is expected of teachers, but at the same time so little is given to them. After all, for their enormous transformative power over their students' lives, it is well known, so the myth goes, that college professors work only a few hours per week and teachers at all grade levels have long summers to relax. Thus, there is a curious tension between the idealization of teaching in the media as a native calling and the day-to-day reality of education practice and policy, fueled by public attitudes, in which teachers are often derided as lazy or inefficient. On the one hand, the public is demanding a rock-bottom price for a workforce that pundits tell them is expendable. Yet the public also wants to cling to the film version of education, where all the teachers are full of special passions and the ability to help every single student move toward monumental life changes.

Getting an education *is* a monumental change, and clearly the pundits believe that more people should have the opportunity to experience such a change. I agree with them. However, the notion that an impersonal and automated approach to education (one that favors efficiency over quality) is a legitimate substitute for those who cannot gain access to places like Harvard or Georgia Tech represents a willingness by the pundits to accept less on behalf of students they will never encounter.

I'm Ready for My Close-Up

When I was in high school, one of my chemistry teachers told me I'd be "best served to be barefoot, pregnant, and in the kitchen as soon as possible after graduation." While I grant that my performance in his class was nothing to brag about, I have never forgotten that moment. It was one of the first times I remember feeling that my gender was the singular framework for how I would be judged. That high school humiliation came racing back as a result of several incidents that occurred during our MOOC. In particular, when one of the threads in the online forum became focused entirely on my clothing.

One evening I logged into the forum discussion page for our MOOC. I noticed that one of the students had initiated a new discussion thread. It was one of the liveliest discussions I had seen on our site. What surprised me was the topic, which on the surface had nothing to do with the course. A debate had ensued about whether my clothing choices for the lecture videos were appropriate. One student, who identified as male, was angry that I would wear something that looked "Indian." "Is she trying to seem ethnic?" he asked. Almost immediately, another student, who identified as female, rushed to defend me. She wrote an extended commentary about women's fashion, explaining that ethnic-inspired clothing was simply stylish. From my perspective as a rhetorician, this was a highlight for the course because it was a sincere discussion about how visual rhetoric works. On the other hand, I was exasperated because this was clearly a gendered criticism.

As far as I have been able to ascertain from conversations with male colleagues who have taught MOOCs, they were never the subjects of a fashion critique. The notion that my sense of fashion, or lack thereof, should be any consideration at all annoys me. In part, I was frustrated because I had given such careful thought to every outfit I wore on camera. In particular, I was concerned about cultural issues.

Before our course began, we invited students during the enrollment period to tag their location on a map we embedded on the course site. From this map we knew we had students on every continent except Antarctica—a widely diverse student population. I did not want to offend people from cultures different from my own. I had made the decision to reach across the Internet to a diverse population of students, and in doing so I felt I had an obligation to be sensitive. I was careful to choose modest clothes (ones with long sleeves and high necklines), and I almost always wore a scarf to cover any open areas around my neck. However, there were some allowances I was unwilling to make. For example, I never covered my head (although, as you will learn, this would have saved me a great deal of money). Generally, I tried to keep my choices casual rather than businesslike, while still maintaining an overall conservative look.

No doubt my former chemistry teacher would have approved of my decision to wear my engagement ring during every taping. Usually I only wear my wedding ring, but I wanted to send a clear signal that I wasn't "available." Distance education professionals at my institution and the campus police had sensitized me to the possibility of harassment from a small minority of the student population, and I wanted to do what I could to avoid any problems. Again, this was never a consideration that my male colleagues mentioned.

Clothing is not merely a matter of fashion or cultural expectation, however. I also was advised to wear clothes that would "pop" on camera. I understood that this was standard video practice, but my male colleagues apparently gave this little thought. Many of them wore the same outfit for every taping.

I also spent more money than usual at my hairdresser's. My hair began to turn gray when I was fourteen; nearing fifty, I'm almost entirely gray, but many people never notice this because I color my hair. During our filming, which occurred over a period of about nine weeks, I couldn't let my roots show at all. The lights in the studio made any amount of gray look like a white stripe and flashed light back to the camera. I was told, gently, that this would be distracting, and I certainly didn't want students focusing on the skunk stripe down the middle of my head when they should be focused on what I was saying. Vanity aside (if vanity is what you call a personal preference regarding one's appearance), there were also issues of continuity. Looking different from taping to taping, especially when the resulting videos belong together in the sequence of online lectures, draws attention to the production of the MOOC, not its educational content. Movie and TV companies pay careful attention to continuity issues, consistent clothing, hair styling, placement of props, and so on, between takes of the same scene, and viewers are alert to any discontinuities and incongruities. This is another way in which the production values of the mass media are infecting education, changing the ways we dress, make ourselves up, and even how we stand or sit.

Facial makeup was another factor I had to pay more attention to than I would have preferred. I have a fair complexion, so the studio lights made me look unhealthily pallid unless I put on more makeup than I usually wear. As

I internalized the need to wear makeup for the tapings (something that even men must become used to when facing a camera), I could not help thinking about makeup as more than a facial prop necessitated by the production process. A little mascara and clear lip balm, my normal routine, now felt lazy and careless. The on-camera me had to be self-consciously poised and polished in a way that started to make the off-camera me seem a bit of a slob. For a brief time, my appearance started to matter to me as much as it apparently mattered to some of my students, and that was following me into my traditional classroom space, too. I was allowing myself to be sucked into celebrity culture—a tiny, ephemeral, niche celebrity culture, but one that detracted from my professional identity as a scholar, nonetheless. My male colleagues expressed some sympathy when I described this feeling, but were obviously bemused. What was the big deal about cameras and lights, they asked? And if a few blowhards were commenting on my appearance, all I had to do was ignore them. None of this is unique to my own experience. There are many notable and troubling incidents of public intellectuals who happen to be women drawing explicitly sexual references, often harassing and even threatening from anonymous commentators. Mary Beard, the United Kingdom's preeminent classics scholar (a superstar professor, no less) has been a frequent target of misogynist harassment.

The fact that there was a forum discussion about my clothing demonstrates that students will be affected by our performance as instructors. When I was first approached about being the instructor for our MOOC, several people commented that I would look good on camera. I was simultaneously flattered and appalled by those comments—in part because few of the people who made these comment also said, "You are an excellent instructor."

How we dress, how our hair looks, our visual charisma on camera, these are things most instructors do not have to consider, nor is the notion of performance—especially at a technically focused research university like mine—but I predict that the arrival of MOOCs, expanded distance education, and blended and flipped classes will change this.

Few instructors today wear traditional business attire to work; indeed, some teach in jeans and T-shirts. Like many of my colleagues, I love the fact that I don't have to give much thought to my clothing if I don't want to. When I left my corporate career, I promised myself I'd never wear pantyhose again. It was a symbolic vow, which marked my passage from a business world that I had come to think of as a performance arena into an academic world that I still regarded as authentic. But as branding issues become a bigger part of MOOCs, I suspect that instructors may find that their clothing choices become more of an issue. I can well imagine university administrators introducing dress codes. And just as the standards between genders vary in the corporate world, female faculty will likely find that the standards are more constraining for them. I remember in the early nineties when casual Fridays became a corporate cultural norm in US business culture. Men usually wore a pair of khakis and a polo-style shirt. Women who wore the same style were often criticized for looking too casual. Even on the other days of the week, men had it easier. A man could own two to four suits and simply change his shirt and tie for variety. A woman couldn't wear the same suit very often without people thinking she was careless (or, if she was already at a certain level in her career, not spending enough money on her wardrobe).

Worse still, I can imagine professors being denied the opportunity to teach a MOOC because they don't "play well" on camera. The old show business saying, "He has a face for radio," comes to mind. Some of the best teachers I had as a student were quirky, nonconventional, and utterly unconcerned with anything except lively discussions. The fact that some of them wore the same outfit three days running was occasionally laughed at, but mostly ignored. Other issues like speech impediments, an inability to make eye contact, a vocabulary peppered with profanity, physical disabilities, difficult to understand accents, obesity—all these things could be a reason to dissuade someone, or deny a person a "role" on a MOOC. And these expectations, seldom expressed overtly, create a minefield that must be negotiated more gingerly by women than men. Where a man may be grizzled or characterful, a woman is likely to be labeled ugly; where a man may be thought handsome, an attractive woman may be too sexy to be taken seriously; where a man talks with authority, the corresponding woman may come across as shrill. At a faculty hiring meeting I once heard a male colleague protest that one of the candidates (a woman) "giggled too much," a manifestation of the noticeable nervousness that I am sure would have been forgiven in a man, and which I am equally sure would have counted against her being put on camera as the face of my male colleague's discipline. Female faculty members will, quite simply, have to negotiate many things that have absolutely nothing to do with teaching.

You Looking at Me?

Aside from personal appearance, I encountered other unexpected issues. Only days before enrollment opened for our course, one of our information technology specialists advised me to change my public email address, because there was a good chance that some students might try to reach me outside the course platform. This, he explained, had the potential of overloading my inbox, making my regular university duties harder to manage.[13]

Ultimately I was convinced to change my primary email address, but not before suffering several days of anxiety about the loss of something that had become part of my personal and professional identity: my name. As an academic, my email address has become part of my professional persona. Typical of many of the IT professionals that I have dealt with, my colleague didn't think through the essential social role played by email addresses and social networking handles. He thought of my email address as a portal through which Internet packets flowed, and was worried only about their volume and legitimacy. To me, my email address was almost as much a part of who I had become as my given name. It was how my professional colleagues and students could find me. I no more wanted to give up my email address than I wanted to change my name when I got married, and for precisely the same reason. Giving up any part of one's identity is difficult. How we name ourselves, and whether we permit others to name us, is critical to our identity and independence.

An administrator colleague of mine shared a story about how she was recently told to change her hyphenated first name in a peculiar context. She has a knack for finding the pop-up booths that offer personalized Coca-Cola cans as novelty collectibles. Where the distinctive Coca-Cola brand name normally appears on the can, you can have your name printed instead— usually, that is, but not in her case. On a shelf above her desk are three cans bearing her name, but on only one is her name hyphenated. On the other two occasions when she tried to get a personalized can, she was told that they could not include "special characters" (except, obviously, they can). Even a space between the two parts of her name would count as a special character, or the two parts would count as two names, and Coca-Cola permitted her to have only one name. It's a strange form of bureaucratic overreach that a soft drink company presumes to tell you what your name should be, but this anecdote shares with my IT colleague's encouragement for me to change my email address a common element: the systems and machines in which we are cogs care only about our identifiers, not our identities. Names are personal possessions. While I have never given my personal contact information to students, I have always expected them to be able to contact me via email, my office phone, and even during virtual office hours I have held using videoconferencing tools. Like many other problems associated with the massiveness of MOOCs, I had never considered how different the faculty-student contact question might be.[14] And I certainly had not considered how teaching a MOOC might necessitate detrimental changes to the ways I interacted with my regular Georgia Tech students—the ones who do pay tuition for their classes with me.

Not long after I changed my email address, conversations about my public accessibility grew more serious. One conversation with an IT colleague led to a consideration of other potential privacy issues that went far beyond my concerns over losing my email address. Might MOOC students feel they could phone me at Georgia Tech? What if a MOOC student lived in Atlanta and decided to drop by my office? Had anyone really considered my general privacy and personal safety? I certainly hadn't considered any of these issues. Suddenly teaching a MOOC seemed potentially dangerous.

What followed was a sobering, hour-long conversation with the chief of campus police. She was astonished that I was being set up unwittingly as a target of harassment. She explained that the more public members of the administration, like the president, routinely had people show up unexpectedly in their offices. Occasionally, former students, even ones who had long ago graduated but were still disgruntled about a poor grade, would appear in faculty offices. She was particularly concerned because I was a woman. She quizzed me about where my office was and where I parked my car. "You don't publicly share your home address, do you?" she asked. Overall, I remember feeling a little sick to my stomach because she sounded so nervous.

After I alerted the director of security for my building, he suggested that I temporarily move my office to a more secure location, in a different building on our campus. To do my job, my real job, not my would-be-star-professor online job, I need students to be able to find me. If I moved my office and then advertised where it was, that would have defeated the purpose of moving. Since my office was already in a semisecure suite, I decided to stay put. At times, teaching a MOOC felt tantamount to being in the FBI witness protection program.

Despite the early concern of others, I decided that all the caution was ridiculously overblown and tried not worry too much about threats that might never come. But then a person began calling me repeatedly. On each occasion, I was out of the office. The caller refused to leave a voice-mail message. Instead he would call the main number of the tutoring center I direct and press members of the staff to provide him with my personal mobile number. He refused to leave messages, saying only that the call was in reference to MOOCs.

Eventually the calls stopped. I was able to discover that they originated in the United Kingdom, which alleviated the serious concerns I was starting to develop about physical stalking, but I never found out who the caller was or his motive. He did stay on my mind when I had to teach in our summer program in Oxford, England, a responsibility that overlapped with the running of my MOOC. Perhaps he was a journalist who wanted a scoop, but journalists generally announce who they are, what they are working on, and for whom they are working. Failing to do any of this was furtive and creepy. Perhaps he was a crank, but the people who heard his voice didn't think he sounded crazy. Perhaps he was a prospective student, but he was asking about MOOCs, not mine in particular. If he was a headhunter, I never made the cut.

The sinister sense of my experience, something that had been totally unanticipated, caused me to wonder about other instructors who might find themselves compelled to teach a MOOC. I often joke that I was "voluntold" to teach mine. I chose to take this on freely, but there were pressures on me to make that choice. In all seriousness, I can imagine other instructors feeling that they have no choice—even if that choice later exposes them to a kind of public life they do not want. Previously, I raised this as a significant concern in the proliferation of MOOCs:

If university administrators are ever to require faculty members to teach MOOCS, would they be prepared to consider the possible implications of requiring someone to become a public figure? Who would be responsible if an instructor is stalked? What if an instructor is harmed? Even if a university can protect an instructor on campus, what happens when he or she goes home? Certainly one might argue that these dangers exist in the traditional brick and mortar environment. However, we do have a screening process that happens with admission. We have more information about our students; in a MOOC students don't even have to provide their name. In traditional face-to-face classes, we can read nonverbal cues, and we often are aware of issues students have before they join our classes (e.g., they have learning or behavioral challenges that require accommodation). Will a university's security and privacy policies transfer to students enrolled in MOOCS? The cost of security is dear—extending to both an institution's ability to provide protection and to the instructor's well-being, should the worst happen. Considering ways to scale up our policies as we scale up our class enrollments is an important administrative responsibility.[15]

Not all my privacy concerns were this sinister. However, deciding to teach a MOOC is not something that should be undertaken lightly.

The Public Face

At the beginning of this chapter, in discussing celebrity culture and the mythos of the superstar professor, I referred to the teacher's role as an authority figure, the face of a discipline or department. When I found myself cast in this role, its implications took me by surprise. I was no longer just *me*; I was First-Year Composition 2.0 and to some people I was Georgia Tech. I also had to come to terms with something that many celebrities understand: thousands of people now thought they knew me.

I am used to being the face of a subject to thirty students at a time, and I relish slowly getting to know them and their getting to know me. It's partial knowledge, but it's genuine. In fact, as Chambliss and Takacs say in their remarkable multiyear study of liberal arts students at Hamilton College, "what matters most in college is who meets whom, and when."[16] To Chambliss and Takacs, the principal factor that influences students academically is the relationship they build with one or two professors. Pedagogy is only a tiny part of that magic; what really counts in the classroom is knowing students' names, and what counts overall are the little things like inviting students to one's home for dinner. None of this transpired with my twenty-two thousand MOOC students. To put this into slightly sharper focus, the total number of students (undergraduate and graduate) enrolled at Georgia Tech in the spring 2013 term was only 19,961. I was teaching the equivalent of our entire campus. What passed as "interaction" in the MOOC was very transactional and impersonal. I mourned the loss of the usual interactions with my students. Still, the MOOC students often thought they knew me as a person.

The irony, though, was that the person they thought they knew was a deliberately watered-down version of the real me. Because I was the public face of my institution and the discipline of composition (if only in the eyes of a few thousand students and for a brief period), I had to withhold myself in ways I did not do with a traditionally sized class. The clothes, the hairstyling, the lights, camera, and action all created a manicured and packaged version of me that was half teacher and half actor, half person and half symbol. Alan Alda would have been proud.

I'm Not a Real Professor, but I Play One in the Classroom

That not all professors are superstar professors should be obvious, but what the public and policy makers often don't appreciate—although the pundits should know this well—is that many "professors" are not professors in the traditional sense at all.

For example, Christensen and Eyring touch on the role of adjunct instructors in their book but don't discuss this role in much depth. They do say that the use of graduate student teaching assistants is a common practice to offset the teaching not done by tenured research faculty, especially those in the sciences. Graduate students are often paid only a fraction of the normal instructional rate; however, they usually benefit from reduced or remitted tuition. Depending on the discipline, teaching responsibilities can vary in graduate school, from leading a small recitation group and tutoring students after larger lecture sessions given by a faculty member to being the instructor of record. The latter was my experience as graduate student in the humanities, an experience that is typical at large research universities.

My own background as a graduate instructor is typical of the contingent experience. Part of my financial aid package in graduate school was my teaching assistantship. In my first semester of graduate school, I was an assistant to an adjunct instructor. The semester after that, I assisted a doctoral student. I also tutored in the university writing center several hours per week. Essentially this was an apprentice system—one that also responded to the state law that mandated a certain number of graduate-level course credits before one could be a full-charge instructor. As early as my second year of graduate school, however, I became an instructor of record and taught either two courses per semester or had some combination of teaching and other instructional responsibilities. For example, I sometimes worked as a writing center tutor in lieu of teaching a second course. In the third year of my doctoral program I was selected to direct the university writing center, a highly sought-after position, because it granted a full release from teaching.

Because I was a teaching assistant, I received tuition remission for every year I was in graduate school; that is to say, I did not have to pay the base price for tuition, although books, student fees, housing, and living expenses were entirely my responsibility. For my master's program tutoring and teaching assistantships I was paid $6,500 for the first year and $8,000 for the second year. For my doctoral program teaching assistantship I was paid $10,000 per year. In addition to that (fortunately) I also received additional funds from private fellowships, and for my doctoral program I received a university fellowship. Even with these fellowships, I never earned more than $25,000 a year. As a consequence of this, I spent my summer months teaching as an adjunct at a local community college and a small private liberal arts university. I usually taught at least two courses each summer; this added approximately $3,600 to my annual income. These were the rates from 1998 to 2004, and my income included no benefits. In 2004, I accepted a three-year, postdoctoral teaching fellowship at Georgia Tech. My teaching responsibilities were three sections of first-year composition (with at least twenty-five students in each section) per semester. My salary was $27,500, but it did include the standard full-time employee benefits package. The postdoctoral fellowship has improved slightly since then—our fellows now earn $37,500, $39,000, and $40,500 in their first, second, and third years, respectively, for teaching three sections of first-year writing or technical communication (still with a minimum of twenty-five students per section).

Whenever I read or hear about the unsustainable increases in college tuition, I reflect on my own experiences as a graduate student teaching assistant, as an adjunct instructor, and as a postdoctoral fellow. The increases in tuition are not contributing to the salaries or professional development of most of the people who are delivering instruction. In the star system of the professoriate, some instructors never get the chance to leave the chorus line or receive the equivalent of a union card that I did. Given that it takes professors six to eight years of postgraduate study to obtain a PhD, the credential needed for work at most universities today, that is a significant investment of time and money. In fact, from a financial standpoint, most recent PhDs have a great appreciation for the cause of lowering student debt, especially if they majored in the humanities.

Christensen and Eyring are absolutely correct in their assessment that graduate programs have created too many people with advanced degrees without the ability to find full-time teaching positions at universities. What they fail to elaborate is why this happens. One reason is that full-time, tenure-track jobs have been replaced with contingent faculty. Another reason is that, as they note throughout their analysis of the historical development of Harvard, graduate students are necessary to teach many of the introductory-level undergraduate courses or must serve as course tutors for large lecture courses taught by full-time faculty. At Georgia Tech this is the reason we have the large Brittain Postdoctoral Teaching Fellowship Program. Because we do not have a traditional English department with an accompanying graduate program, yet we must meet a mandate by our state board of regents to teach first-year writing (a course required at almost every major university), we need qualified instructors. On average, we teach 150 sections of freshman composition every year. The number of full-time, tenure-track faculty members in our school is thirty-four, and most of us teach only four courses per year, many of them advanced courses in our major. Thus, without the postdoctoral fellows, the faculty would have to teach only service courses or general education courses, and it would not be feasible to offer our majors and minors, along with the many advanced elective courses that engineering students and others take to broaden their education. And what is true for my school, with its unusual reliance on postdoctoral teaching fellows, is true for most other schools' reliance on graduate students as instructors of record.

Christensen and Eyring are also correct in their assertion that adjunct professors will work for less money than tenure-track professors, and will do so on an at-will contract basis. When there are no other options, save a career change (unattractive when you've trained so long for a specific career already), adjunct instructors are forced to accept work under whatever terms are offered. To make ends meet, many adjunct instructors work for multiple universities, online and traditional, sometimes teaching up to seven or eight courses in a semester, when they can find the courses to teach. They tend to take on as many courses as offered because there are no guarantees that courses will be available in future semesters. Stress and burnout are extremely common, and since these instructors generally receive no benefits, they have no way to cover their medical expenses if they become ill. In 2013, Margaret Mary Vojtko, a long-time adjunct instructor at Duquesne University, was diagnosed with cancer and lost her job because she couldn't manage the arduous task of teaching so many sections. She was given no severance pay; she had no retirement benefits. She was living in a house she could not afford to heat. Sadly, she died. A couple of weeks later, her lawyer, Daniel Kovalik, published an op-ed about how she died underpaid and underappreciated.[17] And it wasn't as if the university was unaware of her plight. As Kovalik explains, "Duquesne knew all about Margaret Mary's plight, for I apprised them of it in two letters. I never received a reply, and Margaret Mary was forced to die saddened, penniless, and on the verge of being turned over to Orphan's Court." Never mind the inhumanity of a system that creates these conditions: How is it possible for people to work under these pressures and still provide excellent instruction? If all one cared about was the academic bottom line (namely, whether students are learning adequately from such instructors), the question is whether these objectives are being met, and whether they even could be.

Consider the responsibilities surrounding the teaching of even five courses, with all the associated preparation, student conferences, and grading. With only 25 students per course section (and adjuncts routinely have larger class sizes), it is impractical to provide personalized attention to all 125 of them.

And the quick turnover among adjuncts (even with the large pool) creates a lack of continuity and the tendency for the majority of adjuncts to be inexperienced recent graduates who have yet to find more sustainable employment. With many states moving toward exigency measures that would allow them to dismiss permanent faculty (who are paid better and have benefits), the problem is only getting worse.

This line of thinking, then, makes arguments for teaching at scale seem more reasonable. Large lectures, MOOCs, and flipped or blended classes are more efficient uses of high-value professors. Where high-touch interaction is needed (such as problem sessions in a blended setup), doctoral students or low-cost adjuncts can supervise. But for this necessary interaction to be sustainable and of a high quality, an institution needs to provide appropriate incentives. To support the kind of personalized attention and mentoring that Christensen and Eyring cite as being instrumental to the success of BYU-Idaho, one of two things is necessary: either resources must be available to pay the adjuncts adequately, or special cultural norms must be in place that encourage volunteer work. As I shall explain in more detail later, BYU-Idaho's model depends on a form of "labor tithe" from its predominantly Mormon staff and faculty.

Online education comes with further hidden costs that cut more deeply into the savings made by eradicating so many face-to-face instructors. The salaries of support staff must be accounted for, and many of these are technology specialists who earn much higher salaries than junior faculty at traditional universities, and much more than adjunct faculty and graduate teaching assistants.

Merely to enter into these discussions is to accept the premise of books like *Abelard to Apple* and *The Innovative University,* which is that higher education is a business, that issues in higher education can ultimately be understood only by examination through an economic or business lens and resolved by business decision-making techniques, and that teaching is work for hire, with students as customers and courses as commodities for sale. This premise is not entirely wrong, but accepting it wholesale skews the profession of teaching. The outsourcing of higher education in the cheapest possible ways must also be considered as an ethical question. To Christensen and Eyring's credit, they are fully aware of the personal costs of institutionalized professional competition: "For students, universities fashioned after this model are expensive and difficult to access; they also provide preparation more appropriate to advanced study in graduate school than to the workplace. For most faculty, particularly the un-tenured, such universities are pressure cookers that tend to inspire apprehension, envy, and a sense of organizational and intellectual fragmentation."[18] But when an adjunct professor can die in poverty, Christensen and Eyring's subtitle, "Changing the DNA of Higher Education from the Inside Out," rings hollow.

Look Who's Talking

There is a saying: "In theory there is no difference between practice and theory. In practice there is." I wondered what a teaching schedule looked like for someone like Christensen; I phoned the Harvard registrar's office, but could not get any data about his classes. Eyring's background is that of administrator and strategy consultant, and it is unclear from the publicly available information if he has ever taught in a university. It is fairly easy to find state university data, so I was able to obtain the Georgia Tech registration records for DeMillo from spring 2003 to spring 2015. Of his twenty-two classes (seventeen were independent study or research classes, usually with a single student enrolled), two were co-taught with another instructor. Given the standard practice in the Georgia Tech College of Computing of using teaching assistants, it is reasonable to assume that he had this assistance with all classes that were not independent study or research courses. In the spirit of full disclosure, my teaching load is less than some of my Georgia Tech colleagues' because I receive a course release for my administrative duties as director of the Communication Center; even so, from fall 2004 to spring 2015, of the fifty-six classes I taught, only six were independent study or research classes with a single student. One course was co-taught, and for a special study abroad technical writing course I had a teaching assistant (provided by the College of Computing, interestingly). The numbers above do not include the adjunct work (moonlighting in the evenings to supplement my income) I did from 2004 to 2007 (another approximately 240 students), nor does it include my MOOC. Some people might argue that comparing my teaching load with DeMillo's is unfair because our disciplines are different.

For a more direct comparison, I include the teaching data for James Foley, DeMillo's colleague in the College of Computing. For the same period, Foley taught eighty-six classes (fifty-one as independent study or research classes) for a total of 1,135 students. During that time, Foley also served as interim dean for the College of Computing.[19] There are many permutations of teaching responsibilities for instructors, but the stark reality remains that many instructors teach far more than others, even when they have pressing administrative responsibilities. Even though I teach more than some colleagues at Georgia Tech, and I'm guessing more than a tenured professor at Harvard, my teaching load is far lighter than that of my colleagues in nonelite institutions where a four-course-per-semester load is not unusual, and in the case of some colleges a five-course-per-semester load is the norm.

So can anyone speak convincingly about ways to encourage balance for instructors, or about schools in which teaching is the focus, when that isn't his or her experience? The reputation automatically bestowed on faculty at elite institutions lends an easy credibility, no matter the topic. Therefore, the application of reputation matters immensely, because "experts" like Christensen are allowed to drive the conversation about higher education, despite the fact that their experiences do not even begin to approximate those of the vast majority of the people teaching in higher education today. Also, because elite faculty have limited exposure to students (and to an elite group of students at that), it is unlikely that they could understand comprehensively what a cross-section of college-level students want or need. It also bears asking how involved with student life elite faculty members are likely to be. If such a person is spending the bulk of his or her time in a lab, or out on the lecture circuit, or serving on corporate boards, or advising government groups, when is there time to be part of the larger university community?

Without question, those of us grappling with ways we might improve higher education want to make opportunities more accessible and more flexible for those interested in pursuing a degree. However, we are far more likely to find answers if we consult those in higher education who are "in the trenches" than if we limit our conversations to a small number of professors in elite institutions. I grow increasingly concerned that the too-small group of people driving the debate (disruption or revolution, if you like) are not the ones facing the toughest challenges in higher education, the ones getting their hands dirty—and these elite faculty members certainly aren't doing it at the pay rates of many of the millions of higher education instructors,[20] some of whom are as near to despair as was Margaret Mary Vojtko. Even if Christensen, Eyring, DeMillo, and their fellow disruption advocates invited a few people like me to join their small group of innovators, it would not widen the conversation nearly enough.

EIGHT

The Harvard Mystique

Most discussions about disruptive innovation in higher education are motivated by a move toward the democratization of higher education. The irony is that there is, nevertheless, a curious allegiance to a caste system among institutions. Each class of school is presented as fearful of the security of its status from the upstarts and nouveaux riches clambering up from below, while retaining a curiously deferential distance and respect toward their betters above them. Schools should "know their place" by responding to the opportunities of disruptive innovation in different ways.

DeMillo, for example, repeatedly refers to three tiers of institution: the "elites," the "middles," and an unnamed "Lumpenacademe" of community colleges and failing liberal arts colleges, and Christensen and Eyring similarly split the tiers. As long as the public, especially the media, accepts and reinforces this caste system, there is little hope of much change in the reputation-driven tiers. Certainly, full democratization will not occur.

Look at Me! Look at Me!

The idea that a college or university measures elite status by its position in institutional rankings is seldom questioned. Yet at the small liberal arts college I attended for my bachelor's degree, I never once heard anyone worrying that we were not like the elites or even the large state institutions. There was a sense of competition with other small liberal arts colleges, but in none of these cases of friendly, in-group rivalry was there ever a sense of inferiority.

Similarly, my own university's strategic plan calls for Georgia Tech to "redefine the twenty-first-century technology university." Note the word "redefine." It is not enough to "be" that university in other people's eyes;

the concept is to be redefined, and the school is to aspire to be the best in its (self-defined) class. This rejection of others' judgments and rankings, if it became common, would be truly disruptive. A decade ago, things were different. When I first arrived at Georgia Tech, the faculty and administrators referred to the institution half-jokingly as "the MIT of the South," an implicit recognition that there was a substantial gap in status to be closed. I suspect that our colleagues at MIT have never referred to themselves as "the Georgia Tech of New England." Consequently, I am left with the impression that discussions of academic reputation and comparisons among institutions say more about the insecurities and strivings of authors and administrators than the quality of institutions themselves.

The ever-present connection of disruption in higher education with the aspiration of being like the elite institutions is therefore puzzling. Elite status is protected and glorified by the continuous repetition of the argument that any university that isn't among the elite wants to be. Admitting that not every institution need aspire to be among the elite would signify that such a status is not always worth having, and that concept (from the perspective of authors who represent elite institutions) is unacceptable.

Status Envy

Throughout *The Innovative University,* and books like it, the context and structure for almost every other university in the United States is frequently provided through the lens of Harvard's evolution. Past and present Harvard presidents have been given credit for almost everything associated with universities, including the establishment of academic honors, elective courses, standardized testing, intercollegiate athletics, general education, privileging graduate programs, up-or-out tenure, and private fundraising. Of course, Harvard's participation in EdX also places it in the vanguard of yet another trend.

Christensen and Eyring predicate their argument on the notion that many universities try to emulate Harvard. They say there are rare exceptions: Arizona State and Ohio State are two. It is impossible to refute such a vague generalization, but I have never heard this connection made by anyone attending or working in the institutions with which I have been affiliated. In fact, many have distanced themselves from the Harvard model, or were never really so strongly modeled after it in the first place. Certainly Georgia Tech was not.

Sometimes referred to affectionately by students and alumni as the "North Avenue Trade School," the Georgia Institute of Technology throughout its history has strongly used an apprenticeship model, with cooperative education as a principal hallmark for over one hundred years. Long after the transition from regional trade school to internationally ranked research university, Georgia Tech still identifies closely with its hands-on roots. Even its liberal arts offerings are typically infused with technology subjects (for example, Victorian fiction as a lens for attitudes about technology-fueled social change), an approach that far from emulates a traditional liberal arts university.

Christensen and Eyring's recommendation to develop the ambition to court prestigious rankings is, therefore, misplaced. The vast majority of universities will never find themselves near the top of ranking lists. In fact, the only type of improvement that would deserve attention among the "middle" tier of institutions would be to climb ten places in the *US News and World Report*'s annual ranking list of national and regional universities and liberal arts colleges, a feat almost impossible to achieve. Faculty and administrators worry instead about their local reputation and cultivating a network of alumni to help promote their school. Nevertheless, prestige (however impractical to attain) influences people's opinions and choices. As the authors note, many for-profit, online universities have suffered low reputations because they have none of the prestige associated with better-known, nonprofit universities. No doubt the early MOOC developers, most of whom come from the faculty ranks of Stanford, Harvard, and MIT, wanted to link themselves only to other exceptionally prestigious universities. It is in their own best interests to believe in and promote reputation.

Tiers and Careers

In Christensen and Eyring's chapter "Students and Subjects," we are reminded that Harvard students have a special future to look forward to: Harvard students "are more capable than typical college students. They are also more likely to pursue graduate education; that allows them to be more satisfied with a liberal education rather than technical preparation for a career. . . . [These students] are so bright and motivated as to be able to transcend almost any weakness in the educational program."[1] Students elsewhere, by contrast, need excellent programs that emphasize technical preparation for a career: "The challenge for nearly all other universities, in addition to having less to spend than Harvard, is that their undergraduates are much more diverse in both educational objectives and academic abilities. Many of these students will not attend graduate school, so their college experience must include practical career preparation."[2] However, according to the 2015 US News report, "Colleges That Lead to Graduate School," "For plenty of recent college graduates, the lure of graduate school is too strong to resist. On average, about 26 percent of college grads enrolled in a graduate program within one year of graduation, according to the most recent alumni data reported by 402 ranked colleges and universities to US News in an annual survey. That average figure rises to 64 percent at the schools with the highest percentages of graduates pursuing an advanced degree within one year."[3] The twelve schools listed in the report include St. Mary's College of Maryland (a liberal arts college, which tops the list), SUNY-Plattsburgh, and Wayne State University. Seven of the twelve universities are classified as Regional Universities. Not one Ivy League college makes the list. The category Christensen and Eyring dismissed as "nearly all other universities" appears to include colleges that can be more successful than they imagined.

Since most students do not measure up to Harvard (the implicit message being that they should), there should be other, more appropriate tiers for them. As part of their promotion of practical career preparation, Christensen and Eyring discuss the Tennessee Technology Center (TTC) model—one in which students earn certificates rather than degrees. They applaud the TTC graduation rate of 80 percent as evidence that the model customizes instruction for its students. But what does *customize* really mean? Can the typical TTC student envisage having other choices? Imagine that you are a young person from rural Tennessee, and you know no one who went to college except your K-12 teachers. You would quite likely not consider college as an option for yourself, even though you might be capable of succeeding. Going to a technical institute for what amounts to "job training" may seem not only the wisest, but also the *only* path available to you. The resulting certificates will probably help you get a job, but may not add much value to your lifelong earning potential or your ability to grow and adapt as the economy changes and the technical skills you learned become obsolete. I know about Tennessee education firsthand. My first full-time teaching job was at the University of Tennessee in Knoxville, and when I left there I went to the University of Nebraska. One thing both institutions had in common was a population of students who refused to succumb to any notion that a vocational certificate was better than a college degree, but almost universally this was because a teacher or mentor had helped those students imagine themselves as future college graduates.

Thus, many disruption advocates envisage a two-tier career track. In one, more prosperous and academically labeled students move more into a "learning for learning's sake" model of higher education, go to the upper echelon of schools, and choose majors that interest them for their intrinsic value. Upon graduation, their social networks help them find satisfactory jobs to start their careers, and what they learn at college forms a cultural and epistemological backdrop to a future of lifelong learning and adaptation. In contrast, the less well-off are attracted to (or pushed toward) vocational certificates and degrees at technical colleges or the lower-ranked academic institutions, and are encouraged to choose a course of study that maximizes their earnings upon graduation and their projected lifelong return on investment.

The contrast between elite liberal arts education and career-focused education (which I discussed earlier) can also be drawn on a global atlas, with Europe the home of supposedly detached and irrelevant scholarship, and American universities, by comparison, aiming for greater career relevance. In his consideration of why there "are so many philosophy majors," DeMillo talks about his experiences as a visiting professor at the University of Padua, the second-oldest university in Europe, where Galileo was once a professor of mathematics. The descriptions of the city and its university highlight their traditions and heritage, setting the stage for an argument that will focus on the need for change. Throughout his book, DeMillo seeks to portray himself as fearlessly speaking truth to power, and so it seems no accident that he singles out Galileo, a man tried for his role in the scientific revolution during the Renaissance, who was forced to recant publicly his views and spend the last years of his life under house arrest, during which he wrote one of his great works, *The Discourses and Mathematical Demonstrations Relating to Two New Sciences*. After establishing his credentials as a serious discover of truths, DeMillo again begins to place academic life as something rooted in silly traditions, unwilling to consider change: "University traditions are both serious and frivolous, but they are as ingrained as any American traditions. Graduating students—some of them in their underwear—are doused with shaving cream and adorned with laurel wreaths as their classmates chant an ancient, vulgar ditty and their parents look on with embarrassed pride."[4] While this story is humorous, it is a powerful rhetorical move. It strengthens the notion that the higher echelons of the academy worldwide constitute a special club—its traditions strange and even vulgar, but serving to give a sense of identity to those inside the club while excluding those without. It is a place that "has been drawing visitors for centuries."[5] The use of tourism here is another interesting move, making the academy more of a historical curiosity than a place of active learning and scholarship. One need only look as far as Harvard to find a university with a rich set of traditions of the kind that DeMillo ridicules.

Harvard is also invested heavily in research in technology that has direct economic benefits, along with a business school curriculum that provides much more than the jobs training that is acceptable for students who can aspire only to a technical school. Harvard has been keen to expand its Allston Campus to include a sprawling facility for its School of Engineering and Applied Sciences (SEAS), despite concerns from the faculty and surrounding community.[6] After a surprise announcement about the move in 2013, a task force was created to address concerns about the auxiliary campus site—already home to the Harvard Business School. After years of discussions, and with a recent $400 million gift to SEAS, the plans are finally moving forward. No doubt this expansion of the Allston Campus will also further elevate the position of Harvard's Business School, which has a palpable effect on the nation's economy through the career trajectories of most of its graduates. TTC graduates can never hope to benefit from such strong networks of influence, no matter how good their training might be.

And what of the students from the lower tiers of traditional universities? Upper-tier universities are not the exclusive producers of successful scholars and generalists, as some writers often imply by their contrast between Harvard and other schools filled with "typical college students," even though Harvard is as prepared to engage in economic development—and better placed to succeed—than many lower-tier institutions. However, Harvard graduates will likely benefit from more influential networks than will graduates of large state universities.

Rome Never Looks Where She Treads

One of the consequences of the winner-take-all culture of rankings and academic competition is that growth opportunities come to those who need them the least, and that is unlikely to change no matter how many technological innovations or disruptions manifest in higher education. In 2015, Harvard received a $400 million gift from a billionaire alumnus donor, John Paulson. In a series of Twitter posts, writer and social critic Malcolm Gladwell ridiculed the priorities that caused Paulson to donate his money somewhere where it was least needed:

> @Gladwell: If billionaires don't step up, Harvard will soon be down to its last $30 billion. (2:43 PM)
>
> @Gladwell: Next up for John Paulson: volunteering at the Hermes store on Madison Avenue. Let's make this a truly world class [sic] retail outlet! (2:40 PM)[7]

In an article about Gladwell's screed, Sarah Kaplan adds a more measured, but equally critical comment:

> After all, Harvard is only the world's richest university, with a $36.4 billion endowment that's larger than the gross domestic products of Jordan, Bolivia, Iceland, and about ninety assorted other countries. Surely there were other institutions that needed Paulson's support? . . . A small investment team, MG Squared Investments, offered a range of other ways Paulson could have spent the money: associate's degrees for 63,877 Americans, feeding every child in D.C. for two years, mosquito nets that would save the lives of 119,760 children overseas.[8]

No matter what critics may say, donors like to give money to the causes that will most likely be successful, and elite institutions like Harvard are sure bets.

Donors also want to give to programs they believe are high profile; Paulson focused his philanthropy on engineering, not on "so many philosophers," and certainly not on the students getting certificates at TTC.

Leveling the Playing Field

The idea of MOOCs as the grand democratizer of education was a cornerstone of the public relations efforts by those who endorsed them. The promotion of democratization as a result of disruption, however, doesn't ring true. In fact, MOOCs from top-tier schools actually reinforce the current tier structure among institutions.

The top, middle, and bottom tiers will not fundamentally change because of MOOCs or similar technologies, although the bottom tier is likely to experience the most apparent disruption. Elite universities in the top tier will not be disrupted, but will, more likely, take the disruption of others at lower levels as a benefit and opportunity—resulting in their status growing. MOOCs and other allegedly disruptive technologies are worth investigating by the elite-tier schools because they can turn the exposure that these tools create to their advantage in ways that middle- and lower-tier schools cannot. Elite schools, and the pundits associated with them, can afford to play in the most disruptive sandboxes with minimal risk, pitching any failures as important research—and whatever happens in the aftermath of these failures will register as little more than a toy tossed aside for some new plaything, leaving the lower tiers to tidy up the mess.

Niche Institutions

Nevertheless, disruptive innovation may give rise to new small universities to fill niches that existing schools, even the elites, cannot or will not fill. These range from rethought state schools, such as Southern New Hampshire University,[9] to the "unschooling" movement, where college-age students "hack" their education by accessing freely available resources online and exhibit their knowledge through *making* and social activism rather than the writing of papers or taking of exams.

The more extreme examples of this movement are attractive to libertarians and countercultural thinkers. They are yet another way to "stick it to the man." But the contradictions of human nature may counteract any humanitarian or egalitarian motives, as with many idealistic schemes. Consider Carey's hypothesized "University of Everywhere,"[10] which seems very open source and *open*. Carey describes an online space where, he says, "Anything that can be digitized—books, lecture videos, images, sounds, and increasingly powerful digital learning environments—will be available to anyone in the world with an Internet connection."[11] Here again, the "easy" answer is a technological one. But there are at least three problems with this model.

First, the lack of curating and accreditation means that no one can certify the quality of what is learned. It becomes purely an exercise in autodidactic consumerism. Second, and related to the first, a disconnected set of "resources" (that is, online factoids and minilectures) may provide value at the level of local knowledge, but does not help students integrate randomly gathered facts and concepts into deeply connected webs of knowledge. Finally, crowdsourcing, though often effective, has a sinister side. The Internet as a whole has evolved into islands of isolated interests, made only more distinct by recommender systems and agents that give us the information that they compute we want or need and protect us from information that will confuse or confound. This is not a healthy model for higher education. Many people are frustrated by algorithm changes on social media platforms, like Facebook, that decide what gets prioritized in a person's feed. The narrowing possibilities of such an algorithmic approach to what is available in an "open" educational environment could be equally frustrating, and in some cases dangerous. Americans often "tsk-tsk" about how authoritarian governments limit what their citizens can view online, but such limitations can be implemented anywhere at any time.

Location, Location, Elitism

There is an old joke about the famous 1970s New York City nightclub, Studio 54: if you remember it, you weren't there. Nothing grants more cachet and mystique than a velvet rope. Crowds quickly assemble in hopes that they will be deemed special enough to get past the bouncers. Admissions to schools like Harvard work in a similar fashion. So does obtaining a faculty position at most Ivy League schools. The elites don't have to grant tenure very often because, as the argument goes, having an instructorship for three years at Harvard will guarantee you a position elsewhere (BYU-Idaho, perhaps)—so strong is the mystique of having been allowed into the club. Just like at a nightclub, though, there are spaces within the club that are even more exclusive, special party rooms or even entire floors restricted to the most famous of the famous. Having a permanent faculty position at a place like Harvard is much the same. Usually these positions go to people who are already very famous—so famous it is worth having their names on the faculty list, even if they don't actually teach any classes or engage in any research. And once you are member of the "club," you have a place where you can return if you ever need to, even if it is on the heels of a spectacular failure.

For example, after announcing his resignation as president of Cooper Union, Jhamshed Bharucha returned to Harvard, where he had received his doctorate. Bharucha was a highly controversial figure at Cooper Union, reviled by most students, many faculty, and several trustees for depleting the endowment and investing in risky, high-profile, and splashy building projects. During his tenure as president, the board in 2011 began to charge tuition, thus overturning a century of precedent, dating from the Cooper bequest, that guaranteed free education to all students. He described the dismantling of the highly egalitarian culture of Cooper Union as a "disruptive intervention."[12] The reconfigured trustees and succeeding president have since intervened and reversed Bharucha's policies. Bharucha, meanwhile, was offered a position as a visiting scholar at Harvard University in the Graduate School of Education. In the same way institutions like Harvard benefit from being able to take risks other schools would find impossible, those associated with elite schools can also count on an expansive network of fellow elite graduates to offer them "shelter" for a time if they fail elsewhere. Elite networks allow for a privileged few to take bold measures without personal risk. It is no wonder that concepts like disruption originate at places like Harvard. Disruption is something that happens to other people.

NINE

Missionary Creep

One of the more compelling arguments for MOOCs has been the humanitarian benefit. From the beginning, MOOC platform providers and their proponents have touted the idea of free education for all—with what seems a particular nod to the developing world. MOOC instructors would play the role of aid workers and missionaries, transmitting the knowledge—but also perhaps the values and canon—of a privileged Western educational system.

Thomas Friedman was one of the first and most insistent proponents of this ideological argument. In 2012 he quotes Coursera cofounder Daphne Koller as saying, "It will allow people who lack access to world-class learning—because of financial, geographic, or time constraints—to have an opportunity to make a better life for themselves and their families." Friedman then adds his own spin: "When you consider how many problems around the world are attributable to the lack of education, that is very good news."[1] In a later article Friedman ramps up the rhetoric to focus on poverty, a young man with autism, and even the concept of changing the life of an entire village:

> Imagine how this might change US foreign aid. For relatively little money, the US could rent space in an Egyptian village, install two dozen computers and high-speed satellite Internet access, hire a local teacher as a facilitator, and invite in any Egyptian who wanted to take online courses with the best professors in the world, subtitled in Arabic.[2]

My experience teaching a MOOC provided several interactions that reinforce the idealistic motive of educating the world as a development or aid project. We received inspiring messages from students sharing touching personal stories, including one from a quadriplegic who told us the course made him feel equal to "able-bodied" students. Another man told us we "saved his sanity" during long hours of sitting at his wife's bedside during a difficult series of cancer treatments; he even sent us a photo of his wife and her oncology nurse.[3]

We also had the experience of a group of students translating all the materials on our site into Russian—something they did spontaneously. As it happened, one of our postdoctoral fellows was a native Russian speaker, so we were able to confirm that nothing nefarious was happening. While we made jokes about an oligarch possibly co-opting our site for illegal trade negotiations, we were actually more concerned about translation errors that would cause confusion for students. The sense of community within various groups of students was uplifting, and this aspect of my MOOC experience has been the one I've most tried to replicate in my traditional classes.

If we define success in terms of outreach, I would agree that our course was a success, but well-meaning attempts to reach out to the world always raise contradictions. First, not all attempts are successful. For example, while our quadriplegic student's case was heartwarming, some other students with disabilities could not be accommodated and dropped the course. And while we enabled the Russian translators to further enhance the experience of fellow students, as I explained in Chapter 7, my attempts to accommodate some students' cultural expectations about women led to distracting discussions about my choice of clothes. Missionaries and colonists have been aware of similar issues for centuries, sometimes taking the sources of tension and resistance on board as challenges to be overcome and adapted to, sometimes branding them as marks of the native population's ignorance that must be stamped out.

Talk of "teaching the world" naturally fits with the call by many faith traditions to help the poor. Even so, I am struck by how much of the language used to describe higher education is religious. When such a framework is employed, the academy is the church of learning, the faculty members are its monks and priests, and the students are its novices and congregation. Perhaps it is precisely because those people who are leading the call for reform have resided or do reside in the most sacrosanct of institutions that it is easy to slip into the language of religion—a linguistic move that can, arguably, signal the kind of dogma associated with fundamentalism and religious domination.

Another reason for this linguistic move is that religious practice is a framework that many people will understand. When used as an analogy for higher education, it encompasses many subtleties, including the complex and coveted notions associated with transformative experiences, priesthoods with privileged access to the mysteries, and power hierarchies that have endured for centuries by divine right.

The BYU-Idaho Model

BYU-Idaho is an example of a nonelite school that reinvented itself as a way to reach a broader group of students. One of the most striking things about the successes at BYU-Idaho is how much the framework for success depends upon the extensive network of people and facilities associated with the Mormon Church. Without question this was a boon when the university began its online education Pathway pilot.

BYU-Idaho promotes as some of its greatest assets a strong commitment to peer-led programs, volunteer mentors, faculty who work without tenure or rank, and a pool of eager adjuncts willing to work at low cost. The emerging theme here is that this model of success was and is highly dependent upon generosity or coercive exploitation of community members: from the outset the pilot team knew from its research that "effective online learning requires one-and-a-half times as much 'out-of-class' student support as face-to-face courses do."[4] In describing some of their earliest experiences in online education, the faculty and staff at BYU-Idaho realized the value of a hybrid approach. Most universities would face a serious geographical difficulty in providing the face-to-face time (even if only once a week) wherever their online students happened to be. Hiring a workforce that would need to be so diversely scattered would also create challenges. How, for example, would a university oversee the work done by these face-to-face mentors and instructors?

Because of the number of "local church institute buildings, similar to those over which Ricks College president, John Clarke, had presided before coming to Ricks College," the newly renamed BYU-Idaho had unique, perhaps even wholly unprecedented, access to facilities: "To keep the hybrid model of online and face-to-face instruction affordable, the team sought out volunteer retired couples to meet with the students each Thursday night, playing the role of supportive coaches and mentors rather than teachers."[5] Additionally, "BYU-Idaho students on their semester away from the Rexburg campus were recruited to work as volunteers, under the direction of the couples at the institutes."[6] This strategy is particularly questionable from an assessment viewpoint because the student working as a peer-mentor is now being directed by a retired volunteer, who is being directed by a church institute director, who is beholden first to the church's needs, rather than to the university's needs. The degree of separation between the university (and curricular design and assessment) and those providing student support is enormous.

To aid in completion rates, BYU-Idaho also promotes its ability to provide certificate programs in addition to associate's and bachelor's degrees. However, even here it would have been cost-prohibitive and meant acquiring additional accreditation had it not been for the BYU-Idaho link with another church institution, LDS Business College.[7]

In evaluating the success of the BYU-Idaho Pathway project, the writers credit an understanding of why they needed to match the size of the organization to the size of the small test group of Pathway students: the "small team was well matched to the similarly small group of Pathway students. [The online education director] and his colleagues became the de facto academic advisors and parental figures to the fifty young people in the initial cohort. They took the students' phone calls and texts round the clock during that first semester."[8] While this is an example of how they learned to adapt their online offerings by assessing a smaller pilot program, it still depends on a level of engagement that requires either a strong commitment to volunteerism or the willingness to pay someone to serve these functions. Generally, most universities would find it impossible to get faculty and staff willing to answer calls around-the-clock without significant compensation.

For the domestic and international expansion of its Pathway pilot, BYU-Idaho negotiated the use of 230 additional church sites in North America and another 324 in overseas locations.[9] Once again, it is difficult to imagine how it would be possible for other institutions, even Harvard, to achieve this kind of hybrid online instruction. BYU-Idaho is clearly fortunate to have such broad support through its religious affiliation. It is also clear that the school enjoys an ability to promote religion as part of its requirements—all religious schools do this. Given the missionary focus of the Mormon Church, it is not surprising that the First Presidency of the church has been keen to support an expansive online degree program that requires courses in religion during the first two semesters.

Secular universities, which is to say all public universities, cannot count on engendering anything as strong as a faith-based commitment to the institution, which, coupled with the Mormon tenet of tithing, is critical to the continued support of a school like BYU-Idaho. While all universities rely on donor support to offset costs, support must be constantly pursued (usually by a team of fundraising personnel); alumni do not necessarily feel compelled by faith to donate. Since the tithe system in the church is collected and then distributed by the central church administration, BYU-Idaho benefits from not having to focus on fundraising in the ways that secular schools do.

What surprises me most about the case study of BYU-Idaho is the faith-based connection. I am not familiar with any other discussion of disruptive innovation, whether for business, medicine, or education, that relies so strongly on religious zeal, except as a metaphor—even BYU-Idaho is described generally with its denominational dimension sanitized as though it were irrelevant. Perhaps highlighting the religious aspect of the BYU-Idaho story would prompt lukewarm or even negative reactions from policy makers and other constituents who do not accept a particular (or any) religious tradition. You have to read the book in depth (not just skim the charts, graphs, and summaries) to understand just how important religion is in this case. The Church of Jesus Christ of Latter-day Saints and BYU-Idaho are inextricably intertwined, and this oversight has been vital to the singular transformation of the school. Christensen and Eyring's morality tale is therefore a parable that cannot be applied to other campuses as readily as they imply.

Hogwarts and Other Tropes

DeMillo focuses on foreign universities to frame many of his arguments about higher education—choosing some of the most venerated institutions as examples and often using elaborate religious imagery to make his arguments. His religious references begin, of course, with the title of his book—Abelard was himself a priest, although one who would break his vows for the love of Héloïse. From Abelard we move quickly to the idea that universities are ritualistic places very like religious institutions—framed as hallowed halls or cathedrals. In the opening pages of the book, DeMillo describes universities this way:

> If academic life is impenetrable to the layman, it is because universities are designed to be mysterious. The mystery begins with rituals that are especially forbidding to outsiders. Universities are by definition associated with rites of passage—passage from adolescence to adulthood, from apprentice to master. European universities were originally medieval and monastic, and American institutions inherited their traditions . . . This [religious] influence is most obvious in the academic rituals like commencement ceremonies that involve scepters and other magical icons and imagery, monastic gowns and regalia, and the ritual intonation of passages that confer special status to conferees. An academic processional resembles nothing as much as monks solemnly filing into chapel for Mass. It is not accidental that literature is filled with deliberately blurred boundaries between religion, wizardry, and scholarship.[10]

Wizardry? Perhaps this is a reference to the Harry Potter books so familiar in contemporary culture; any allusion to Hogwarts as a model for universities would conjure a certain opinion, especially from all the Muggles who will never make it to the other side of Platform Nine and Three-Quarters, into the exclusive world of magical education. Here the religious imagery is meant to isolate those within the academy—even make them seem ritualistic in ways that are suspiciously heretical. Are they, perhaps, worshiping the false gods of scholarship? To describe universities this way, especially in the opening pages of the book, sets a clear tone: universities are mysterious, cloistered places that need to be exposed through revelation. He promises this in the opening lines of his book: "The gears and levers of a modern university are hidden from public view by a curtain, and I want to help you peek behind it."[11]

Later in his book, in a chapter titled "The Computer in the Cathedral," DeMillo revisits some of the religious imagery that focuses readers on the "otherness" that, in his view, isolates the modern university. As in earlier chapters that focus on the founding of universities in a historical context, readers again find themselves in Europe (this time in Spain), another way of creating a kind of distance—a rhetorical move that takes readers back to the "old world," to situate our current problems in the contemporary world as having deep roots. DeMillo begins with language about a "story," the same folksy stylistic approach we've seen earlier in the text. In this case, his story purports to help readers understand how universities began to "divert funds from education to support an industrial policy that was not otherwise sustainable."[12] In his "story," professors have become "martyrs and heroes" who answer these otherwise unsustainable needs.

To this end, DeMillo takes readers to the Universitat Politècnica de Catalunya (UPC) in Barcelona. He uses his first couple of paragraphs to establish the exotic nature of the place, another way of establishing the university, in this case UPC, as *other*. Amid the cloistered gardens, we pass a building that houses the "schools of informatics, telecommunications, and engineering" to find a "fountain at the base of a broad staircase on which is perched the four-story Rectorat."[13] At this point, I really did expect a Harry Potter-type character to appear behind a secret entryway—such was the rhetorical buildup to the "inner world" of UPC. But part of me knew that the denouement would be prosaic. I spent a summer teaching at UPC myself, and found the steep hill I had to climb each day from the subway station to be the most notable feature of the environment. Nonetheless, I was captivated by DeMillo's description—feeling as if this were some magical place that I had missed during my time there. We learn that the Rectorat is "literally the rectory of a former church, Torre Girona," and that "inside the church is one of the world's most powerful supercomputers ... [the] Mare Nostrum."[14] Readers then find the only photograph used in the book: the Barcelona Supercomputing Center. The photo that DeMillo uses is one that magnifies the mysterious feeling he is using to talk about the supercomputer. He could have used another photo for a very different rhetorical effect—one that focused on technology rather than religious imagery. Mare Nostrum is just a machine, after all. Instead, DeMillo escalates the "cathedral" trope by using a dimly lit view that incorporates the original architecture of the deconsecrated chapel. The narrative sounds very much like a cathedral tour script, calling attention to "the background music: Gregorian chants and medieval motets, played through speakers hidden in the architectural detail of the chapel. . . . Chanting monks are what you hear."[15]

Next we are introduced to a graduate student named Francesco, who is described as looking monkish in his sandals and hooded sweatshirt. Instead of pews full of monks, the lights are turned up to reveal the supercomputer in its glass case, visible through iron gates. DeMillo is very moved by the presentation, saying that even "jaded technologists are not prepared for the experience."[16] Anyone who has ever toured a cathedral and peered through the screen to the sacristy directly behind the altar will find DeMillo's description of seeing Mare Nostrum very familiar. The scene described is definitely meant to sound like a sacred place.

Then the story moves to an administrator's office, and DeMillo says, "I know we are back in the world of mortals. . . . The show is over. Now it is time to talk about one of the most expensive university laboratories in the world." Ironically, because he is using the same "show-like" rhetorical moves, he adds a coda: "But we have been properly prepared, because we have experienced Mare Nostrum as it was intended to be experienced." Having willingly succumbed to the propaganda clearly designed to be part of a tour of Mare Nostrum, DeMillo has learned through his experience how to use the same tools throughout his own "storytelling." From invoking Abelard to the constant references that describe universities as mysterious places considered sacred by the few who have access, DeMillo creates an implicit argument that the hallowed walls must be torn down—that "we" (the outsiders) must gain access to that which is denied us. But it isn't only walls that must be destroyed—the inner sanctums of truly elite universities are not a problem because they are so special; they are, we are told time and again, what other institutions strive to be. No, it is the nonelite institutions that no longer need their walls—literally they no longer need even physical spaces. Instead, they need to become open cathedrals, virtual ones, where anyone with a computer can take tours whenever and however he or she likes. As with so much propaganda, the idea used to create discontent or panic is the very thing that gets protected. The masses need not think about tearing down Harvard or Stanford, but they should storm the campuses of nonelite institutions and demand immediate and revolutionary change *there*.

Family Values

In addition to their focus on disruptive technology, Christensen and Eyring also make a controversial argument about disruption, namely, a return to values-based education, saying, "For the sake of both its own survival and society's good, the traditional university needs to reengage on the subject of values and renew its commitment to character development. The moral void created by the secularization of higher education is a critical weakness."[17] They continue by arguing that students *want* help developing their personal values. (They seem to be talking about traditional college students, not the midcareer professionals returning to college who are now the majority.) If a student chooses a religiously affiliated university, he or she is more likely to be open to such instruction—although arguably there are students who are forced into such institutions by their parents or guardians. The biggest difficulty in providing this instruction is that it is highly personal. Exactly whose values will be taught?

Christensen and Eyring cite former Harvard president, Derek Bok, who said, "It is perfectly possible to teach moral reasoning or prepare students to be enlightened citizens without having instructors impose their personal ideologies or policy views on their students."[18] They continue by explaining that this is one of the functions of tenure, and that tenured professors, especially, bear the responsibility for "not just bringing new discoveries into the classroom, but also for transmitting cultural memory and mentoring."[19] In fact, Christensen and Eyring argue that this is one reason for maintaining a tenured professorate.

Is tenure really a protection for faculty who attempt to answer this call? In secular institutions, it could be a career-ending choice. Recently, professors have lost tenured positions because they have voiced publicly (even outside the classroom) their personal values. University boards are increasingly concerned that such speech is indicative of what professors might say in the classroom. One example is the University of Illinois Urbana-Champaign's 2014 revocation of a job offer to Steven Salaita because of political views he expressed on Twitter.[20]

Historically, professors have weighed in on policy and political debates, but today they often do so not in magazines or newspapers, but on social media. Again, the massive reach of social media gives access to a much wider range of people who are not part of the community most directly involved, but who believe that they have every right to call for the disciplinary action, even for dismissal of a professor. Online campaigns can create immense pressure on university boards. As in other ways, Christensen and Eyring may enjoy more protection from such responses because they are at institutions where such pressure is more easily resisted. Harvard, in fact, has built its reputation, in part, on vocal faculty who regularly make public comments about controversial issues. To think, however, that a politics professor at a small state school, for example, enjoys the same protections as a superstar professor at Harvard is shortsighted and irresponsible. The vast majority of faculty across the United States, tenured or not, must be very careful about anything they say, in class or outside class, that ventures into the subjective.

Christensen and Eyring also argue for professors who can act as surrogate parents and family members for students, believing that great professors can and should involve themselves in the personal lives of their students. They also believe that parents will appreciate this: "The would-be life-changing professor cannot be value neutral or laissez-faire. The university community that expects parents to pay the high cost of its expansive campus cannot entirely refuse to act *in loco parentis*."[21] While they cite circumstances in which mentoring became personal, like the approval of a student's marriage, students today, and their parents, would likely consider such unsolicited "advice" both inappropriate and unwelcome. We can turn to technology for the reason. Students in college today need far less *in loco parentis*, because they are much more closely attached to their parents via their mobile phones and social media. One of the greatest classroom challenges I have faced in recent years is students receiving calls and texts during class—these calls and texts often come from their parents, and students feel strongly that it is absolutely appropriate (even essential) that they respond immediately.

All this attention to the insinuation of professors into students' personal lives would be highly unlikely in most online classes, which raises the question how technology can be used to change the way students think about more than just their coursework.

The Academic Missionary

Another way that religious imagery is being used to support the oft-promoted humanitarian benefits of providing free higher education to the world is more veiled than the obvious connections we see in books about higher education disruption. The focus on elite institutions as the hallmark of what is needed to improve higher education also leads to the idea that the best content will also come from the faculty who teach in such places. Again, this was a key promotional point for MOOCs—only the most elite schools were asked to create the first MOOCs, and only a limited number of other schools participate now. The result of such a small pool of resources is that the content choices (that is, the canon for any given discipline) is limited to what a select group of people feel the rest of us should know about a subject:

> As MOOCs attracted media attention, there was an intense focus on elite American universities providing their special brands of education to domestic and foreign masses . . . [The] rhetoric has continued to focus on elitism while simultaneously promoting a kind of egalitarianism. . . . Still, there are only a limited number of "providers" of courses, and these providers have been specially chosen, not because these institutions necessarily have the best instructors, but because those instructors happen to be part of the instructional staff of one of these elite schools. . . . People who believe in a "best instructor" model would likely argue that there is no need to have hundreds of different approaches to teaching a given subject. However, this argument does not account for the vast knowledge base available in many subjects. Such a model also does not account for vast cultural differences and considerations that must be part of the design of courses meant for students outside the traditional American university systems or, for that matter, for the diverse set of students enrolled in American universities.[22]

However, if the goal is not only to provide educational opportunities to underserved communities, but also to carefully control what content is promoted, then the enterprise begins to look like a missionary effort—one in which what I've called *academic colonialism* becomes an important component. If content (a selective academic canon) is determined by an exclusive group of elite academics, then we are in danger of creating situations like the nineteenth-century Indian boarding schools, which were touted as a way to educate Native American children, but were actually designed as a system of cultural repression. There are, of course, many other examples of missionary work that quickly become the kinds of colonialism that seek to make populations more homogenous. In the case of MOOCs, well-intended though providers may be, there is a particular danger of homogeneity. To avoid this problem, we must design MOOCs and other online resources in ways that decrease the possibility of cultural repression. We must include a larger pool of instructors; we must be more critical about course design, recognizing the ways each of us perpetuates particular cultural hegemonies; and we must consider ways to leverage MOOCs to broaden rather than narrow the canon in any academic field.

Such broadening of the MOOC curricula and accepted practices, instructional approaches, and cultural participants will produce generations of students who will be better able to consider (and with luck solve) problems. If expansion fails to occur, we risk a dangerous kind of single-mindedness that could significantly diminish innovation and limit problem solving in every sector of our lives.

Preventing ourselves from thinking and writing about universities using religious language is an important step to improving higher education. The rhetoric of religious language serves only to codify the current divisions between *kinds of education* and *kinds of institutions*, and it reinforces a model that risks being more or less (although, perhaps more virtual) the same model we currently have, albeit more narrowly defined.

Balancing My Parentheses

There is an adage that writing is never finished; it is only due. I frequently bring this up with graduate students who are nearing the end of work on their dissertations. I can tell the time is ripe to let go when they begin to talk about separating from their dissertation in language that mimics that of a person about to break up with a romantic partner. At some point you have to acknowledge that one more attempt at making the project better (adding one last source, for example) isn't really going to make much difference in the final outcome; it is time to call it quits and say goodbye.

However, when I opened Kentaro Toyama's 2015 book, *Geek Heresy: Rescuing Social Change from the Cult of Technology*, I realized I needed to delay breaking up with my own book. Among the flood of recent books on the future of higher education and technology in schools, Toyama's resonated with me. Like me, he writes from the perspective of an insider. Like me, he entered into a technologically utopian project with great ambition and optimism (more so than I did, actually). And like me, he has been chastened by the outcomes. Also like me, he takes issue with the simplistic technological optimism that drives much of the thinking on the future of education and which waves away reasonable objections as Luddism.

And then, by happenstance, an email arrived announcing an event that felt very much like déjà vu. There was to be another Georgia Tech town hall meeting, and, as things transpired, I was to become involved in another educational technology project. Between Toyama's book and these events, I knew I needed to write one more chapter.

Virtual Paradise Lost

Toyama's book, *Geek Heresy*, offers a very different picture of technology's effects on education from the views of the disruption pundits. Toyama speaks with authority. Having cofounded Microsoft Research India, he spent five years designing technologies to help improve educational opportunities for struggling populations. He knows what it is to get his hands dirty. As a computer scientist he understands why so many people embrace technology as the panacea for almost any problem, but he has also learned that technology can merely amplify situations—good or bad.

Toyama explains that as early as 1913, the idea that technology would fundamentally change education systems was already a strongly held belief. Thomas Edison was convinced that motion pictures would replace textbooks because people remembered only a small portion of what they read, but would remember most of what they saw in a film. In the 1930s, Benjamin Darrow thought radio would bring education to the masses. Similar arguments came with the advent of television. However, as Toyama observes, "All of these predictions sound achingly similar to today's claims for digital technology. If history is a guide, new technologies will be absorbed by schools, but will do little in the end to advance education. . . . Maybe, though, digital is different. After all, real education involves two-way instruction, while broadcast media is only one-way. Don't computers, the Internet, and social media offer something that television doesn't? Rigorous studies say no."[1] Yet, he argues, it is difficult to avoid getting caught up in utopian thinking—even when your own experiences demonstrate the flaws in certain ideas. One reason that people cling to certain technology-inspired utopian views is that it is in their best interest to do so:

> Toward the end of my five years in India, I had a glimpse of a hypothesis. I knew there was a way to make sense of the apparent contradiction whereby isolated successes weren't easy to replicate elsewhere. But since I worked at a company whose soul was software, I kept wanting to see that technology prevail. I felt disloyal doubting its value. As Upton Sinclair said, "It is difficult to get a man to understand something, when his salary depends upon his not understanding it." I needed some distance. I needed some time. . . . Technology's impact was

complex, but I hoped to find a concise way to understand when it was good, when it was bad, and when we could know in advance.[2]

Toyama goes on to explain that he left Microsoft for a fellowship at the University of California–Berkeley, where they not only build new technologies, but also study how those technologies affect people. It is this commitment to reflection that must underpin the work we all do—whether the focus is on education or another area.

Toyama is not the only technologist who is asking tough questions about whether educational technologies are the answer to the complex issues facing higher education. Clay Shirky, who teaches the theory and practice of social media at New York University, now questions the efficacy of laptops and other devices in traditional classrooms. Many colleges require students to own a laptop, but a growing number of instructors wish laptops and other such devices would disappear from their classrooms. On the one hand, many instructors like being able to have students work on projects in class, and some projects necessitate computer access. On the other hand, students often engage with their laptops in ways that are counterproductive and distracting. This behavior is not new, of course. Long before there were laptops, iPads, and smartphones, students (myself included) found ways to ignore what was happening in class: completing crossword puzzles was not so different from playing Angry Birds; passing notes was not so different from messaging; and doing work for another class remains just as possible without a laptop as it is with one. The problem is not the abundance of technology. The problem is the lack of meaningful engagement. Nevertheless, even technology-friendly instructors are beginning to ban laptops and similar devices from their classrooms. As Shirky elaborates:

> I'm a pretty unlikely candidate for Internet censor, but I have just asked the students in my fall seminar to refrain from using laptops, tablets, and phones in class. I came late and reluctantly to this decision—I have been teaching classes about the Internet since 1998, and I've generally had a laissez-faire attitude towards technology use in the classroom. This was partly because the subject of my classes made technology use feel organic, and when device use went well, it was great. Then there was the competitive aspect—it's my job to be more interesting than the possible distractions, so a ban felt like cheating.

And finally, there's not wanting to infantilize my students, who are adults, even if young ones—time management is their job, not mine. Despite these rationales, the practical effects of my decision to allow technology use in class grew worse over time. The level of distraction in my classes seemed to grow, even though it was the same professor and largely the same set of topics, taught to a group of students selected using roughly the same criteria every year. The change seemed to correlate more with the rising ubiquity and utility of the devices themselves, rather than any change in me, the students, or the rest of the classroom encounter.[3]

Considering the challenges instructors face inside traditional classrooms, why would we expect more motivation and engagement from students enrolled in a MOOC or MOOC-like course? In a MOOC, the distractions are built in—notifications of mail, social media updates, or news alerts, and so on, can come at any moment on the same screen that is commanding attention to course material. Additionally, by their very design, MOOCs are almost always (even the most interactive ones) a form of the "sage on the stage" lecturing approach, an approach that impedes engagement. It is difficult enough to hold the attention of a student who knows you can see what he or she is actually doing. Is there, then, any real hope of holding the attention of a student who has no accountability? This is surely one of the reasons students drop out of MOOCs. It isn't simply that it's easy to quit because the MOOC is free. The ease of quitting is also a reflection of the fact that no one will really notice what you do or don't do. Even in online courses where students pay, and where they do have virtual contact with an instructor, the degree of separation still allows for a lack of accountability. When I think back to the conversations I had with the computer science students I was teaching during my MOOC planning, it was their insistence that they wanted a classroom experience that resonates most with me. Having to show up to class, because of the attendance policy, was a kind of motivation—they were accountable to me. If they skipped my class, they might run into me on campus later. We had a relationship. Likewise, I have said many times that I mourn the students I never had in my MOOC—of nearly twenty-two thousand, I meaningfully connected with only about ten. There was little chance I would ever run into any of them in person, and even if I did, I would never know it.

Human Connection

When people ask me about my work in writing centers, I tell them that I was drawn to tutoring because it is everything I love about teaching, minus the parts I don't love. When I sit down to tutor, it is a one-on-one connection. While there is usually some form of technology employed (a printed text, a video or photograph on a smartphone, a simulation on a laptop, etc.), the most important thing I do is have a conversation—this is true even if tutoring is done virtually. Tutoring is often called coaching because the main task is to help the student move toward greater success, but do so with his or her own unique set of skills. The best tutoring always focuses on helping students get where they want to be in ways that work best for them. If the student is getting tutored for a particular assignment, the goal is often to get a good grade, but that isn't always true. There are students who are already going to get a good grade, but they want to find ways to make the assignment more stylistically their own. There are other students who know their grade will not be good, but they want to get as much from the assignment as possible in order to do better on future assignments. Sometimes students come for tutoring when there is no assignment at all. Technology becomes an issue only when students don't know how to make a device or program do what they want it to do. Technology is just a tool. Technology itself does not create meaningful connections between people.

When we lose sight of technology as a tool, it becomes easy to elevate it to a status that makes it the be-all and end-all to our problems. As Toyama argues, "many techno-centric projects hold themselves out as a comprehensive solution, or, if they are slightly more careful, as a primary solution that requires a little human support."[4]

Yet direct human support is the element most sought after in education. The smaller the ratio between faculty and students, the costlier education becomes. Throughout history, those who could afford it have employed private tutors for their children. Around 343 BC, Philip II of Macedon sought the best possible tutor for his son, Alexander the Great. That tutor was Aristotle. The best private schools have always touted their low faculty-to-student ratios. However, the vast majority of people cannot afford private tutors or even private schools, and the institutions charged with providing public education are always challenged to find ways to educate large numbers of students at the lowest possible cost. Therefore, each time a new technology is introduced, there are those who quickly champion that technology over less efficient alternatives. Trying to find "the easy answer" is part of human nature. However, as Toyama explains, "It may seem obvious that packaged interventions work best when leaders, implementers, and beneficiaries have great amounts of heart, mind, and will. But plenty of smart, influential people behave otherwise, as if spreading technologies and packaged interventions indiscriminately were the way to cause social progress. To do so, though, is to make an idol of the easy part and neglect the rest—the finding or nurturing of the right heart, mind, and will."[5] Technological innovation will continue to dominate discussions about improving higher education, but without the human connection, technology will at best provide a temporary Band-Aid for our problems; at worst it will create new problems that are more harmful that the original ones.

Same Time, Same Channel

Nearly three years to the day, I received an email invitation for a second town hall meeting to discuss educational innovation: Help Transform Georgia Tech's Educational Landscape: A Town Hall on the Educational Innovation Ecosystem. I was beginning to wonder if I might be in the movie *Groundhog Day*, where Bill Murray's character repeatedly experiences the same day in his life. On the one hand, I wanted to stay very far away from the meeting; on the other hand, I felt utterly compelled to attend. In the previous meeting I had needed to reschedule a student conference; now I was concerned that I might not make it to my noon class on time—the tension between education and strategizing about education is ever-present.

I resolved to go, and so it was that I headed back to the Klaus Building in our College of Computing, the same location as for the first MOOC town hall, and where I had been the first person ever to use the "secret" technology-enabled classroom to teach my most recent course. The Klaus Building gives one the feeling that technology is the foundation of everything. In keeping with this, the topic and the panelists looked very familiar; only one of the six was not directly connected to a technological field.

While many aspects of this second town hall felt the same, my expectations differed in two significant ways: I was no longer naive enough to think that it had nothing to do with me; and I was there because I was fascinated by what would be said, not because I thought it was a command performance. This time, I did not sit in the back row, but I was still not comfortable enough to ask any questions. The room was less full, but many of the people who have become familiar to me as a result of my MOOC experience were present. Many members of the upper administration were there, although, once again, most of the college deans and our president were absent.

For a second time we had been called together to hear about the efforts to secure Georgia Tech's place as a leader in educational innovation. While MOOCs were no longer the only focus, the role Georgia Tech has played in MOOC development was omnipresent. There was even a call for professors interested in MOOCs to submit proposals. We were assured that online education would *not* be the only path to innovation, and yet the discussion returned repeatedly to how we could use technology to develop a complete set of markets. Overall, the message was that Georgia Tech should be at the forefront of educational technology because it is the Georgia Institute of *Technology*.

What followed was less scripted than the town hall three years earlier. The panel and Q&A presentation were more like a traditional academic conference than a pep rally. The scene was set to project a more traditional scholarly atmosphere, complete with slides full of Venn diagrams and bullet points. Despite these rhetorical shifts in presentation style, the spotlight was, once again, squarely focused on the Center for 21st Century Universities, and the emphasis remained on being first in a kind of race to the top, a race that was very much about winning the reputation game in educational innovation.

Once again there was a return to an often-used train metaphor: "The train has left the station, and we need to be on it and driving it." The first part is evidently true. No modern university can ignore the opportunities that technology gives us to improve education, even though any predictions today of where technology is heading will probably seem laughably anachronistic in ten years' time. But what the second part of the metaphor means is debatable. We should use evidence from our pilots and experiments, including mine, to shape and moderate our goals and plans for the future. But we should be wary lest the intoxicating desire to drive innovation results (to extend the train metaphor) in everyone running out of steam. And while these reflections were prompted by a local event involving my colleagues, they apply, of course, to all universities that seek to improve educational quality and access through technological means.

Four years on, I am unwilling to accept that we might not have the track built, or even more significantly, that we have no idea where we are headed. We are quite able and should be inclined to engage in the necessary reflection about what we have already done—in some cases spectacularly and in other cases not so successfully.

We need to assess what works and what does not. As Toyama observes, "Seeking mass dissemination of technology for its own sake is a waste of resources and often counterproductive."[6] At the town hall, one of the audience members asked why we are not more engaged in high-quality educational research, saying that without it everything we had done with MOOCs amounts to little more than mythology. The "we" in the question referred to Georgia Tech, but it could equally have been generalized to refer to higher education in general. DeMillo, who was the panelist representing C21U, responded by saying that such efforts needed to be distributed across campus, that we needed a critical mass, and that the hope was that a new educational innovation ecosystem would offer answers. Many people, myself included, were not inspired by that answer. Hadn't C21U been responsible for coordinating efforts surrounding educational innovation and its assessment for the past five years? Another audience member pressed by asking about milestones and measures of success—what had they been and what were they now? One answer from a panelist shifted us to reputation—since our admissions were up, potential students clearly saw us as innovators. It's true that Georgia Tech has a great reputation for return on investment, one of the oldest and most robust co-op and internship programs, not to mention the longstanding reputation for having top programs, especially in engineering. But none of these laudable features have depended for their reputation on technological innovation of the kind that was being promoted.

Not mentioned at the town hall meeting were several remarkable innovations that *have* been introduced on our campus which have palpably changed the educational climate and culture. The year before our first

MOOCs launched, we opened a state-of-the-art learning commons building (affectionately referred to by the students as the CULC) that contains not only classrooms, but also academic support centers and flexibly scheduled conference rooms and study spaces. It has become the center of gravity of the undergraduate student experience. Partly in response to the explicit introduction of teamwork-building exercises and project work into many of our courses, but in part also because of the needs and expectations of a new generation of students, the CULC is full of students at all hours studying in peer-led groups and working on team projects.

Also at the same time that the first MOOCs were developed, we introduced our first major living-learning community for resident undergraduates, "Grand Challenges," in which students live and work together on proposals to address some of the major sociotechnical challenges facing humanity. We don't expect them to succeed, but the aim is for them to understand through experience that leadership in modern society is more about listening to others, communicating with them and influencing them, identifying big problems, and carving off achievable miniprojects. Current plans are exploring the development of several more communities like Grand Challenges with slightly different identities.

As a final example, the Create-X innovation ecosystem has revolutionized students' access to entrepreneurial opportunities. Some students merely use this to experiment in our maker space, the Invention Studio. Others go on to learn about entrepreneurship. And still others are sponsored to spend a summer launching a start-up, and receive mentorship and rigorous criticism. The InVenture Prize is an annual competition involving teams of student inventors that culminates in a live televised final. The Vertically Integrated Projects program, which has spread to many other universities, places undergraduates, graduate students, postdocs, and faculty on large, interdisciplinary research teams that work on significant applied problems through which students learn more, about not only their academic disciplines, but also teamwork, communication, and essential work skills.

None of these Georgia Tech programs is unique—any more than our MOOCs. Other universities have created learning commons and have rethought what a student commons should be, but ours is state-of-the-art and has transformed student culture. Living learning communities have been around for decades, but ours dovetail well with our goal to prepare students for technology leadership. Other universities are moving into innovation, entrepreneurship, and the maker movement, but nowhere does this appeal more strongly to the interests and aspirations of students than at a school like Georgia Tech. What all these programs have in common, even those which depend on technology in part, is that they are designed around learning through meaningful interpersonal interactions, not commodification of learning at scale. They are innovations too, arguably more institutionally sustainable and life-changing for our students than are MOOCs.

What's in It for Me?

For me, the most important moment in the second town hall came when the moderator pressed the panelists to say why a junior faculty member should consider working with innovative teaching methods, and how that decision might affect promotion and tenure decisions. With my own tenure review on the horizon, I was eager to hear what a public statement on this might be. There was agreement that research within the new education innovation ecosystem will be important, but a caution that everyone with tenure would need to acknowledge the importance of this work and support junior colleagues who were engaged in pedagogical innovation. It was not the bold statement I had hoped to hear, but at least the issue was finally being discussed publicly.

During the Q&A session at the 2013 State Higher Education Executive Officers policy conference (where I was so anxious about sharing the stage with the vice chancellor), I was asked if I had any ideas about ways to engage more faculty in innovative pedagogy. I said there, and in a number of conferences since, that the way to encourage innovative pedagogical experimentation involves creating innovative paths to tenure. Otherwise, junior faculty will be best advised to steer clear of such projects because they take a great deal of precious time away from the work that will result in positive tenure decisions.

In the same way that administrators want to promote and protect the reputation of their institutions, faculty members want to promote and protect their own professional reputations. Until educational experimentation and scholarship are valued in every discipline, the faculty will focus on building a reputation in traditional ways, which will mean, for many, avoiding any meaningful work related to teaching.

The two town hall meetings were more than convenient narrative book-ends to my MOOC experience; they animate the inconvenient truth that "culture eats strategy for breakfast." This is a proverb often attributed in management literature to Peter Drucker, but possibly apocryphal.[7] Strategy can co-opt the latest, "sexiest" technology: MOOCs yesterday, something even newer tomorrow. In contrast, culture can be viewed as a set of self-sustaining, change-resistant power structures and systems of perverse incentives that the people in an organization cannot help but follow. In particular, whether an innovation gains traction and sticks depends on what incentives its intended adopters receive. Yes, say faculty members, polish your shiny toys and use them to promote our institution, but leave me alone to get on with my career. Yes, let us set a visionary target, the educational technology "ecosystem," but do not chastise us for not articulating what our previous "experiment" was designed to show, and do not challenge us for evidence that it is working when no one knows what "working" means. Yes, let us encourage educational innovation in bold, massive course design projects, but do not presume to consider them as equivalent to mainstream research projects from which faculty can gain professional credit. It was endearing and frustrating for the second time in three years to watch administrators I respect fail to acknowledge these contradictions between technology imperatives and human interests. And yet could one expect more? The allure of technology-based strategies coupled with good intentions is almost impossible for technology-focused minds to resist. And when these efforts are in response to a perceived "tsunami" of disruptive change, there is precious little time for reflection and assessment.

What's in It for Us?

The self-interest of the average faculty member and the incentives that faculty respond to are at the heart of common contradiction. We often complain about technology we are required to use as part of our job, but we are unwilling to have a say in its selection, design, and deployment. There doesn't seem to be adequate time or justification to take this on when it is presented as another task force or committee assignment that draws us away from our principal responsibilities of teaching and research. Somebody else can do it. After my MOOC experience, I was gun shy and inclined to adopt this attitude. I resolved not to say yes to any more requests until my career was better established.

Unlike MOOCs, learning management systems (LMSs) like Blackboard, Desire to Learn, and Canvas are the kind of technology that *does* affect all faculty members. All institutions except the smallest and most traditional colleges use them, so they are an inescapable reality for those involved in university instruction. LMSs are repositories for course materials, access points for communication between members of the class, and grade books. In some cases, they also provide mechanisms for blogging, for synchronous and asynchronous interactions, and wikis—to name a few. They are also closed systems that provide the appropriate amount of protection to meet federal guidelines for student privacy.

Georgia Tech has recently embarked on an evaluation of such providers, with an eye toward changing from the open source platform, Sakai, which we have been using for several years. At the second town hall, the former technology specialist who advised my MOOC asked me to serve on the LMS Faculty Advocates Committee and to pilot one of the LMSs under consideration. As if listening to someone else, I heard myself agree. My reason was the same as the one that guided me to say yes to the MOOC project: I didn't want to hear about it second- or third-hand, and I didn't want the decision to be in the hands of people who do not teach students regularly.

When offers like this are made to us faculty members to participate in the creation of our work environment, we should rise to the challenge. Our technology environment should not be something to complain about like the weather; we should play a role in changing it. If, as future users, we refuse to engage with administrators who may not understand the full slate of requirements in practical terms, then decisions are likely to be guided by the bells and whistles that are promoted by the manufacturer as the most innovative features available—even if those features won't work or aren't really needed. Toyama argues, "Modern society fetishizes technocratic devices, but it is a human finger on the on-switch and a human hand at the controls,"[8] and I would add that it is very important to consider whose finger or hand is controlling those devices.

I think most administrators are trying to make the best possible decisions to support faculty needs, student needs, and institutional needs, but they will be wooed by technologies if they are not apprised of the practical issues about which they are unaware. For this reason, faculty can no longer isolate themselves in their labs or in their classrooms.

Won't Get Fooled Again

Over the past three years, I have been interviewed many times. Whether the interviewer is a journalist or a graduate student working on a dissertation project, one question always seems to come up: "What is the future of MOOCs?" Often there is a follow-up question: "Will technology ever allow for education platforms that replace our current universities?" I have avoided making predictions because technology changes so fast. If someone had told me in 2004, when I began working at Georgia Tech, that an object not much larger than a deck of cards would allow me to have real-time video conversations with my nephew, Jason, who lives in the Netherlands, I would have said that was still a science fiction concept—something I could imagine happening, just not very soon. In 2010, I upgraded my iPhone and suddenly video-conferencing on a handheld device was part of my everyday life. While I remain reticent about predictions, the time has come for me to answer these two often-asked questions.

MOOCs have failed, I believe, to be superior to a traditional classroom experience, but they have contributed to some changes that will continue to influence teaching methods. However, MOOCs have inspired professors, myself included, to incorporate more technology into their teaching practices. For example, if bad weather causes a campus closure, my MOOC experience has helped me be more comfortable recording a lesson and distributing it to my students. I am confident about arranging for class to meet virtually—something that is fairly easy with fifteen to thirty students. MOOCs have taught me to use technology to free up class time for those things that only I can do with students. I can record minilectures with foundational information, which means I do not have to use class time to disseminate that material. Instead, I can sit with students while they work on their projects, giving them immediate feedback. Using technology in this hybrid way is not something I would be doing as much, perhaps not at all, if I hadn't taught a MOOC. Developing a MOOC for tens of thousands of students across the globe also forced me to think more critically about cultural inclusion when I design my traditional courses. Essentially, MOOCs helped me consider my teaching practices through a new lens, which allowed me to revise (or augment) my practices to strengthen my effectiveness as a teacher.

In the broader educational landscape, MOOC providers have already shifted their advertising to focus on skills-based, career-enhancing courses or on personal development courses. Given that many of the original MOOC students already had college degrees, it is easy to understand how a focus on supplemental education has proven more reflective of market demand. From a business standpoint, MOOC providers always needed to find ways to generate revenue, and with the new focus on specializations they have found customers willing to pay for their services. For example, Coursera's specialization tracks offer bundled courses in particular areas, like learning a computer coding language for a low cost. The four-course specialization with a capstone project in Python coding costs $415. Gone are the "everything is free and open" days of the earliest MOOCs, but at these prices, I expect this model to continue to draw interested students.

As for traditional universities that grant degrees, I predict another shift. Dropping the "M" and the first "O" in MOOC, we begin to move toward another lasting legacy of MOOCs. More robust online courses will continue to be part of distance education. There will always be students for whom a residential college experience is impossible. The online master's degree in computer science at Georgia Tech is a good example.

In another decade, I believe that MOOC will disappear as a term, but not as a concept. I think the term will continue to carry connotations of what didn't work. Therefore, MOOC providers, and their marketing teams, will look for a new way to brand what they offer.

Whatever does or doesn't happen to MOOCs is not the most critical question. The critical question is about disruption in higher education. *Disruption* (also perhaps under a new name) will continue to have champions, and those champions will continue to push for a two-tiered system of education. I fear my opportunity to study a broad range of subjects as part of a liberal arts curriculum will become a luxury available only to a small number of students who can attend elite schools. Critics might argue that nothing much will change because our most successful innovators attended elite schools, but that isn't always true—Steve Jobs attended Reed College, a small liberal arts college in Oregon. The notion that those who attend elite schools should have access to the broadest possible education, while everyone else should be limited to only an education that prepares them for a specific job, is a notion that is in direct opposition to the American promise of opportunity for all. Limiting opportunity limits our potential as country. A diversity of educational experience yields a population that is rich with creative ideas and approaches. The most difficult problems will not be solved without original ideas, and such originality does not easily spring forth from skills-based training. Disruption in its most extreme manifestation is, it turns out, best described as a natural disaster like a tsunami—a thing that will cause indiscriminate destruction.

Notes

ONE. THE RHETORIC OF PUNDITRY

Epigraph: Ken Auletta, "Get Rich U," *New Yorker*, April 30, 2012.

1. Clayton M. Christensen, *The Innovator's Dilemma: When New Technologies Cause Great Firms to Fail* (Brighton, MA: Harvard Business School Press, 1997).

2. Clayton M. Christensen, "Disruptive Innovation," *Key Concepts* (September 10, 2014), http://www.claytonchristensen.com/key-concepts/.

3. Thomas Friedman, "Come the Revolution," *New York Times* (May 16, 2012).

4. Laura Pappano, "The Year of the MOOC," *New York Times* (November 4, 2012).

5. Thomas Friedman, "Revolution Hits the Universities," *New York Times* (January 27, 2013), http://www.nytimes.com/2013/01/27/opinion/sunday /friedman-revolution-hits-the-universities.html.

6. Tamar Lewin, "Master's Degree Is New Frontier of Study Online," *New York Times* (August 18, 2013).

7. Andrew Rice, "Anatomy of a Campus Coup," *New York Times Magazine* (September 16, 2012), http://www.nytimes.com/2012/09/16/magazine/teresa -sullivan-uva-ouster.html.

8. Matthew Watkins, "Free Freshman Year? Texas State Hopes to Try It Out," *Texas Tribune* (September 10, 2015), https://www.texastribune.org/2015/09/10 /free-freshman-year-texas-state-will-try-it-out/.

9. Donald A. Schon, *The Reflective Practitioner: How Professionals Think in Action* (New York: Basic Books, 1983).

10. *Purdue Online Writing Lab,* https://owl.english.purdue.edu/owl/.

11. *Excelsior Online Writing Lab,* http://owl.excelsior.edu.

12. "Study: Who Teaches MOOCs?" *Inside Higher Ed* (October 26, 2015), https://www.insidehighered.com/quicktakes/2015/10/26/study-who-teaches -moocs#.Vi4Yvx3RwqQ.mailto.

13. Scott Jaschik, "MOOC Mess," *Inside Higher Ed* (February 4, 2013), https://www.insidehighered.com/news/2013/02/04/coursera-forced-call-mooc-amid-complaints-about-course.

14. Scott Freeman, et al., "Active Learning Increases Student Performance in Science, Engineering, and Mathematics," *Proceedings of the National Academy of Sciences of the United States of America* 11, no. 23 (2014), http://www.pnas.org/content/111/23/8410.

15. Alezu Bajak, "Lectures Aren't Just Boring, They're Ineffective, Too, Study Finds," *Science Insider* (May 12, 2014), http://news.sciencemag.org/education/2014/05/lectures-arent-just-boring-theyre-ineffective-too-study-finds.

16. Clayton M. Christensen and Henry J. Eyring, *The Innovative University: Changing the DNA of Higher Education from the Inside Out* (San Francisco: Jossey-Bass, 2011).

17. Richard A. DeMillo., *Abelard to Apple: The Fate of American Colleges and Universities* (Cambridge: MIT, 2011).

18. Christensen and Eyring, *Innovative University,* 399–401.

19. Ibid., 401.

20. DeMillo, *Abelard to Apple,* x.

21. Ibid., ix.

22. Ibid., xi.

23. Ibid., xii.

24. Ibid., xiii.

TWO. MY EDUCATIONAL JOURNEY

1. Karen J. Head, "Left Off," *Inside Higher Ed* (June 25, 2015), https://www.insidehighered.com/advice/2014/06/25/essay-academics-who-are-advised-leave-their-associate-degrees-their-cvs.

2. "Occupational Outlook Handbook: Postsecondary Teachers," United States Department of Labor: Bureau of Labor Statistics (2015), http://www.bls.gov/ooh/education-training-and-library/postsecondary-teachers.htm.

THREE. SWEET DISRUPTION

1. "Nontraditional Undergraduates/Definitions and Data," *US Department of Education Institute for Educational Sciences: National Center for Educational Statistics,* https://nces.ed.gov/pubs/web/97578e.asp.

2. Kelly Rolstad and Kathleen Kesson, "Unschooling, Then and Now," *Journal of Unschooling and Alternative Learning* 7, no. 14 (2013): 33, http://jual.nipissingu.ca /wp-content/uploads/sites/25/2014/06/v72142.pdf.

3. Jill Lepore, "The Disruption Machine: What the Gospel of Innovation Gets Wrong," *New Yorker* (June 23, 2014), http://www.newyorker.com/magazine /2014/06/23/the-disruption-machine.

4. Andrew A. King and Baijir Baatartogtokh, "How Useful Is the Theory of Disruptive Innovation?" *MIT Sloan Management Review* (September 15, 2015), http://sloanreview.mit.edu/article/how-useful-is-the-theory-of-disruptive -innovation/?utm_source=twitter&utm_medium=social&utm_campaign =featsept15.

5. J. L. Austin, *How to Do Things with Words* (Cambridge: Harvard University Press, 1975).

6. Aaron Bady, "The MOOC Moment and the End of Reform," *New Inquiry* (May 15, 2013), http://thenewinquiry.com/blogs/zunguzungu/the-mooc-moment -and-the-end-of-reform/.

7. DeMillo, *Abelard to Apple,* 41.

8. Thomas Friedman, "The Professors' Big Stage." *New York Times* (March 6, 2013).

9. Ken Auletta, "Get Rich U," New Yorker (April 30, 2012), http://www .newyorker.com/magazine/2012/04/30/get-rich-u.

10. David Brooks, "The Campus Tsunami," *New York Times* (May 4, 2012).

11. DeMillo, *Abelard to Apple,* 41.

12. Ibid., 42.

13. Ed Folsom and Kenneth M. Price, eds, *The Walt Whitman Archive,* http:// www.whitmanarchive.org.

14. Eric Spiegel, "MOOCs Will Change the University Business Model: The Opportunities—and Risks—in the MOOC Business Model," *Wall Street Journal* (October 15, 2013), http://www.wsj.com/articles/SB1000142405270230456100457 9135363266072976.

15. Michael Stratford, "Corinthian Closes for Good," *Inside Higher Ed* (April 27, 2015), https://www.insidehighered.com/news/2015/04/27/corinthian-ends -operations-remaining-campuses-affecting-16000-students.

16. Ibid.

17. Karen J. Head, "Of MOOCs and Mousetraps," *Chronicle of Higher Education: The Wired Campus* (blog), February 21, 2013, http://chronicle.com /blogs/wiredcampus/of-moocs-and-mousetraps/42487.

18. Karen J. Head, "Sweating the Details of a MOOC in Progress," *Chronicle of Higher Education: The Wired Campus* (blog), April 3, 2013, http://chronicle.com /blogs/wiredcampus/sweating-the-details-of-a-mooc-in-progress/43315.

19. DeMillo, *Abelard to Apple,* 116.

20. Lawrence Lessig. *The Future of Ideas: The Fate of the Commons in a Connected World* (New York: Random House, 2001): 238.

21. Stewart Brand, *The Media Lab: Inventing the Future at MIT* (New York: Viking, 1987): 202.

22. Ibid., 34.

23. Karen J. Head, "Massive Open Online Adventure: Teaching a MOOC Is Not for the Faint-hearted (or the Untenured)," *Chronicle of Higher Education* (April 29, 2013), http://chronicle.com/article/Massive-Open-Online-Adventure/138803/.

24. Karen J. Head, "The Hidden Costs of MOOCs," in *Invasion of the MOOCs,* ed. Steven Krause and Charlie Lowe (Anderson, SC: Parlor Press, 2014): 53.

25. "An Open Letter to Professor Michael Sandel from the Philosophy Department at San Jose State U," *Chronicle of Higher Education* (May 2, 2013), http://chronicle.com/article/The-Document-an-Open-Letter/138937/.

26. Henry Ford, *My Life and Work* (Garden City, NY: Doubleday, Page & Company, 1922).

27. Daniel Chambliss and Christopher Takacs, *How College Works* (Cambridge: Harvard University Press, 2014): 136.

28. DeMillo, *Abelard to Apple,* 132.

29. Ibid., 125.

30. Ibid.

31. Ibid., 133.

32. "The University of Cambridge: The Age of Reforms (1800–82)," *British History Online,* http://www.british-history.ac.uk/vch/cambs/vo13/pp235–265.

33. "University College London." *Wikipedia,* https://en.wikipedia.org/wiki /University_College_London.

34. Christensen and Eyring, *Innovative University,* 325.

35. Ibid., 330.

36. Ibid., 338.

37. Ibid., 385.

38. Ian Bogost, "MOOCs are Marketing: The Question Is, Can They Be More?" *Blog: Ian Bogost* (July 18, 2012), http://bogost.com/writing/blog/moocs_are _marketing/.

39. Carl Straumsheim, "Place Your Bets," *Inside Higher Ed* (August 22, 2014),

https://www.insidehighered.com/news/2014/08/22/unsettled-ed-tech-market
-investments-are-easily-found.

40. Osvaldo Rodriguez, "The Concept of Openness Behind c- and x-MOOCs (Massive Open Online Courses)," *Open Praxis* 5 no. 1 (2013): 67–73, http://openpraxis.org/index.php/OpenPraxis/article/viewFile/42/12.

41. *Excelsior Online Writing Lab.*

42. DeMillo, *Abelard to Apple*, 56–57.

FOUR. TALKING BUSINESS IN HIGHER EDUCATION

1. Christensen and Eyring, *Innovative University*, 3 (emphasis mine).

2. Margaret Spellings, "A Test of Leadership: Charting the Future of US Higher Education," *US Department of Education website*, http://www2.ed.gov/about/bdscomm/list/hiedfuture/reports/final-report.pdf.

3. Christensen and Eyring, *Innovative University*, 4.

4. Harry Lewis, *Excellence without a Soul: How a Great University Forgot Education* (New York: Public Affairs, 2006): 195.

5. DeMillo, *Abelard to Apple*, 103–4.

6. Christensen and Eyring, *Innovative University*, 214.

7. Jeff Schweers, "Firm Will Get about $186 Million to Manage UF Online," *Gainesville Sun* (March 27, 2014), http://www.gainesville.com/article/20140327/articles/140329618.

8. *Western Governors University Website,* http://www.wgu.edu.

9. Matthew Watkins, "Free Freshman Year?"

10. Scott Jaschik, "Breakup in Florida," *Inside Higher Ed* (September 14, 2015), https://www.insidehighered.com/news/2015/09/14/u-florida-renegotiating
-contract-pearson-provide-services-uf-online.

11. DeMillo, *Abelard to Apple*, 55.

12. Ibid., 56.

13. Ibid., 102.

14. Philip G. Zimbardo, *The Stanford Prison Experiment Website,* http://www.prisonexp.org.

15. Valerie Strauss, "Trump University: Why the NY Attorney General Called It a Scam," *Washington Post* (August 8, 2015), https://www.washingtonpost.com/blogs/answer-sheet/wp/2015/08/08/trump-university-why-the-n-y-attorney
-general-called-it-a-scam/.

16. Karen J. Head, "Lessons Learned from a Freshman Composition MOOC,"

Chronicle of Higher Education: The Wired Campus (blog), September 6, 2013, http://chronicle.com/blogs/wiredcampus/lessons-learned-from-a-freshman-composition-mooc/46337.

17. Judith Shapiro, "The Digital Natives Are Restless," *Insider Higher Ed* (August 21, 2014), https://www.insidehighered.com/views/2014/08/21/essay-technology-issues-facing-students-and-faculty-members.

18. Lee Gardner and Jeffrey R. Young, "California's Move Toward MOOCs Sends Shock Waves, but Key Questions Remain Unanswered," *Chronicle of Higher Education* (March 14, 2013), http://chronicle.com/article/A-Bold-Move-toward-MOOCs-Sends/137903/.

19. "eCore: Georgia's College Core-Curriculum . . . Online," *University System of Georgia Website,* https://ecore.usg.edu.

20. Karen J. Head, "Here a MOOC, There a MOOC: But Will It Work for Freshman Composition," *Chronicle of Higher Education: The Wired Campus* (blog), January 24, 2013, http://chronicle.com/blogs/wiredcampus/here-a-mooc-there-a-mooc-but-will-it-work-for-freshman-composition/41883.

21. Head, "Of MOOCs and Mousetraps."

22. TyAnna K. Herrington, "Who Owns My Work? The State of Work for Hire in Academics in Technical Communication," *Journal of Business and Technical Communication* 13, no. 2 (1999): 125–53.

23. Quoted in Herrington, 143.

24. Christensen & Eyring, *Innovative University,* 52–53.

25. Jonathan Wai and Jenna Goudreau, "The 105 Smartest Public Colleges in America," *Business Insider* (September 30, 2015), http://www.businessinsider.com/the-105-smartest-public-colleges-in-america-2015–9.

26. DeMillo, *Abelard to Apple,* 64.

27. Ibid., 93.

FIVE. WELDERS, NOT PHILOSOPHERS

1. Barack Obama, "Remarks by the President on Opportunity for All and Skills for America's Workers," *White House: Office of the Press Secretary,* https://www.whitehouse.gov/the-press-office/2014/01/30/remarks-president-opportunity-all-and-skills-americas-workers.

2. Zac Anderson, "Rick Scott Wants to Shift University Funding Away from Some Degrees," *Herald Tribune* (October 10, 2011), http://politics.heraldtribune

.com/2011/10/10/rick-scott-wants-to-shift-university-funding-away-from-some-majors/.

3. Alice Ollstein, "Why Marco Rubio Owes Philosophy Majors an Apology," *Think Progress* (November 10, 2015), http://thinkprogress.org/politics /2015/11/10/3721387/why-marco-rubio-owes-philosophy-majors-an-apology/.

4. George Anders, "That 'Useless' Liberal Arts Degree Has Become Tech's Hottest Ticket," *Forbes* (July 29, 2015), http://www.forbes.com/sites/georgeanders /2015/07/29/liberal-arts-degree-tech/.

5. DeMillo, *Abelard to Apple*, 150–51.

6. Ibid.

7. Karen J. Head, "Are MOOCs the Future of General Education?" *Journal of General Education: A Curricular Commons of the Humanities and Sciences* 63, no. 4 (2014): 244–55.

8. John K. Waters, "Taking Competency-Based Credentials Seriously in the Workforce," *Campus Technology Website* (May 11, 2016), https://campustechnology .com/articles/2016/05/11/taking-competency-based-credentials-seriously-in-the -workforce.aspx.

9. "Response to Friedman," *Term Paper Warehouse,* http://www. termpaperwarehouse.com/essay-on/Response-To-Friedman/283337.

10. "2015 PayScale College ROI Report," *PayScale,* http://www.payscale.com /college-roi.

11. DeMillo, *Abelard to Apple*, 35.

12. "2015 PayScale College ROI Report."

13. Kristin Bailey, "Georgia Tech Reaches New Heights in Academic Success," *Georgia Tech News Center* (November 9, 2015), http://www.news.gatech.edu /2015/11/09/georgia-tech-reaches-new-heights-academic-success.

14. G. Christensen, et al., "The MOOC Phenomenon: Who Takes Massive Open Online Courses and Why? (working paper), http://www.meducation alliance.org/sites/default/files/the_mooc_phenomenon.pdf.

15. Kathryn Zickuhr and Aaron Smith, "Home Broadband 2013," *Pew Research Center* (2013), http://www.pewinternet.org/2013/08/26/home-broadband-2013.

16. Karen J. Head, "Left Off."

17. Gardner and Young, "California's Move Toward MOOCs."

1. Claudia Buchmann, Vincent Roscigno, and Dennis Condron, "The Myth of Meritocracy? SAT Preparation, College Enrollment, Class, and Race in the United States," *Paper Presented at the Annual Meeting of the American Sociological Association* (August 10, 2006), http://citation.allacademic.com/meta/p104558_index.html.

2. Andrew S. Belasco, Kelly O. Rosinger, and James C. Hearn, "The Test-Optional Movement at America's Selective Liberal Arts Colleges: A Boon for Equity or Something Else?" *Educational Evaluation and Policy Analysis* (June 12, 2014), http://www.collegetransitions.com/wp-content/uploads/2014/02/Belascoetal_TestOptional.pdf.

3. Head, "Massive Open Online Adventure."

4. "Bloom's Taxonomy," *Wikipedia,* https://en.wikipedia.org/wiki/Bloom's_taxonomy.

5. "CCCC Position Statement: Principles for the Postsecondary Teaching of Writing," Conference on College Composition and Communication (2015), http://www.ncte.org/cccc/resources/positions/postsecondarywriting.

6. Ibid.

7. Christensen and Eyring, *Innovative University,* 353.

8. Ry Rivard, "Humans Fight over Robo-Readers," *Inside Higher Ed* (March 15, 2013), https://www.insidehighered.com/news/2013/03/15/professors-odds-machine-graded-essays.

9. Les Perelman, "Construct Validity, Length, Score, and Time in Holistically Graded Writing Assessments: The Case against Automated Essay Scoring (AES)," in *International Advances in Writing Research: Cultures, Places, Measures,* ed. Charles Bazerman, et al. (Anderson, SC: Parlor Press, 2012): 121–50.

10. "NCTE Position Statement on Machine Scoring," National Council of Teachers of English (2013), http://www.ncte.org/positions/statements/machine_scoring.

11. Head, "Are MOOCs the Future of General Education?" 149–50.

12. Thomas C. Reeves, "How Do You Know They Are Learning? The Importance of Alignment in Higher Education," *International Journal of Learning Technology* 2, no. 4 (2006): 294–309.

13. Head, "Here a MOOC, There a MOOC."

1. *Scientific American Frontiers*, Public Broadcasting Service, http://www.pbs.org/saf/alan.htm.

2. "Alan Answers," *Scientific American Frontiers,* Public Broadcasting Service, http://www.pbs.org/saf/alanswers.htm.

3. "The Flame Challenge," *The Alan Alda Center for Communicating Science,* http://www.centerforcommunicatingscience.org/flame-challenge-2015/.

4. Richard Feynman, Robert B. Leighton, and Matthew Sands, *The Feynman Lectures on Physics: The New Millennium Edition* (New York: Basic Books, 2011).

5. DeMillo, *Abelard to Apple,* 126.

6. Ibid.

7. Ibid., 145.

8. Michael Sandel, *Justice: What's the Right Thing to Do?* (New York: Farrar, Straus & Giroux, 2010).

9. "An Open Letter to Professor Michael Sandel from the Philosophy Department at San Jose State U," *Chronicle of Higher Education* (May 2, 2013).

10. Reid Hoffman and Ben Casnocha, *The Start-up of You: Adapt to the Future, Invest Yourself, and Transform Your Career* (New York: Crown Business, 2012).

11. Head, "The Hidden Costs of MOOCs," 48.

12. Head, "Massive Open Online Adventure."

13. Ibid.

14. Head, "The Hidden Costs of MOOCs," 48.

15. Ibid., 49.

16. Chambliss and Takacs. *How College Works,* 16–17.

17. Daniel Kovalik, "Death of an Adjunct," *Pittsburgh Post Gazette* (September 18, 2013), http://www.post-gazette.com/Op-Ed/2013/09/18/Death-of-an-adjunct/stories/201309180224.

18. Christensen and Eyring, *Innovative University,* 135.

19. This data was obtained from the Georgia Tech Office of Institutional Research and Planning Self-Service Website and is available to the public only by request.

20. "Occupational Outlook Handbook: Postsecondary Teachers."

1. Christensen and Eyring, *Innovative University*, 347.

2. Ibid., 348.

3. "Colleges That Lead to Graduate School," *US News & World Report* (June 2, 2015), http://www.usnews.com/education/best-colleges/the-short-list-college /articles/2015/06/02/10-colleges-that-lead-to-graduate-school.

4. DeMillo, *Abelard to Apple*, 144.

5. Ibid.

6. "Allston: The Killer App," *Harvard Magazine* (February 5, 2013).

7. Malcolm Gladwell, "@Gladwell," Twitter (June 3, 2015).

8. Sarah Kaplan, "Malcolm Gladwell: 'If Billionaires Don't Step Up, Harvard Will Soon Be Down to Its Last $30 Billion,'" *Washington Post* (June 5, 2015), http:// www.washingtonpost.com/news/morning-mix/wp/2015/06/05/malcolm-gladwell -if-billionaires-dont-step-up-harvard-will-soon-be-down-to-its-last-30-billion/.

9. Marc Parry, Kelly Field, and Beckie Supiano, "The Gates Effect," *Chronicle of Higher Education* (July 14, 2013), http://chronicle.com/article/The-Gates-Effect /140323?cid=trend_right_wc.

10. Kevin Carey, *The End of College: Creating the Future of Learning and the University of Everywhere* (New York: Riverhead Books, 2015).

11. Ibid., 5.

12. Tom McElroy, "Jamshed Bharucha Resigning as President of Cooper Union," *Huffington Post* (June 10, 2015), http://www.huffingtonpost.com/2015/06/10 /jamshed-bharucha-resigning_n_7558284.html.

NINE. MISSIONARY CREEP

1. Thomas Friedman, "Come the Revolution."

2. Thomas Friedman, "Revolution Hits the Universities."

3. Karen J. Head, "Inside a MOOC in Progress," *Chronicle of Higher Education: The Wired Campus* (blog), June 21, 2013, http://chronicle.com/blogs /wiredcampus/inside-a-mooc-in-progress/44397.

4. Christensen and Eyring, *Innovative University*, 311.

5. Ibid., 310.

6. Ibid., 312.

7. Ibid., 314.

8. Ibid., 318.

9. Ibid.

10. DeMillo, *Abelard to Apple,* 4.

11. Ibid., 3.

12. Ibid., 65.

13. Ibid.

14. Ibid.

15. Ibid, 66.

16. Ibid., 67.

17. Christensen and Eyring, *Innovative University,* 354–55.

18. Ibid., 356.

19. Ibid., 355.

20. Scott Jaschik, "Out of a Job," *Inside Higher Ed* (August 6, 2014), https://www.insidehighered.com/news/2014/08/06/u-illinois-apparently-revokes-job-offer-controversial-scholar.

21. Christensen and Eyring, *Innovative University,* 357.

22. Karen J. Head, "The Single Canon: MOOCs and Academic Colonization," in *MOOCs and Open Education Around the World,* ed. Curtis J. Bonk, Mimi Miyoung Lee, and Thomas C. Reeves (New York: Routledge, 2015): 12–20.

EPILOGUE

1. Kentaro Toyama, *Geek Heresy: Rescuing Social Change from the Cult of Technology* (New York: Public Affairs, 2015): 8.

2. Ibid., 16.

3. Clay Shirky, "Why I Just Asked My Students to Put Their Laptops Away," *Clay Shirky* (blog), September 8, 2014, https://medium.com/@cshirky/why-i-just-asked-my-students-to-put-their-laptops-away-7f5f7c50f368.

4. Toyama, *Geek Heresy,* 110.

5. Ibid., 112.

6. Ibid., 108.

7. "Did Peter Drucker actually say "culture eats strategy for breakfast"—and if so, where/when?" *Quora,* https://www.quora.com/Did-Peter-Drucker-actually-say-culture-eats-strategy-for-breakfast-and-if-so-where-when.

8. Toyama, *Geek Heresy,* 73.

Bibliography

"2015 PayScale College ROI Report." *PayScale.* http://www.payscale.com/college-roi.

"Alan Answers." *Scientific American Frontiers.* Public Broadcasting Service. http://www.pbs.org/saf/alanswers.htm.

"Allston: The Killer App." *Harvard Magazine* (February 5, 2013).

Anders, George. "That 'Useless' Liberal Arts Degree Has Become Tech's Hottest Ticket." *Forbes* (July 29, 2015). http://www.forbes.com/sites/georgeanders/2015/07/29/liberal-arts-degree-tech/.

Anderson, Zac. "Rick Scott Wants to Shift University Funding Away from Some Degrees." *Herald Tribune* (October 10, 2011). http://politics.heraldtribune.com/2011/10/10/rick-scott-wants-to-shift-university-funding-away-from-some-majors/.

"An Open Letter to Professor Michael Sandel from the Philosophy Department at San Jose State U." *Chronicle of Higher Education* (May 2, 2013). http://chronicle.com/article/The-Document-an-Open-Letter/138937/.

Auletta, Ken. "Get Rich U." *New Yorker* (April 30, 2012). http://www.newyorker.com/magazine/2012/04/30/get-rich-u.

Austin, J. L. *How to Do Things with Words.* Cambridge: Harvard University Press, 1975.

Bady, Aaron. "The MOOC Moment and the End of Reform." *New Inquiry* (May 15, 2013). http://thenewinquiry.com/blogs/zunguzungu/the-mooc-moment-and-the-end-of-reform/.

Bailey, Kristin. "Georgia Tech Reaches New Heights in Academic Success." *Georgia Tech News Center* (November 9, 2015). http://www.news.gatech.edu/2015/11/09/georgia-tech-reaches-new-heights-academic-success.

Bajak, Alezu. "Lectures Aren't Just Boring, They're Ineffective, Too, Study Finds." *Science Insider* (May 12, 2014). http://news.sciencemag.org/education/2014/05/lectures-arent-just-boring-theyre-ineffective-too-study-finds.

Belasco, Andrew S., Kelly O. Rosinger, and James C. Hearn. "The Test-Optional Movement at America's Selective Liberal Arts Colleges: A Boon for Equity or Something Else?" *Educational Evaluation and Policy Analysis* (June 12, 2014). http://www.collegetransitions.com/wp-content/uploads/2014/02/Belascoetal _TestOptional.pdf.

"Bloom's Taxonomy." *Wikipedia*. https://en.wikipedia.org/wiki/Bloom's _taxonomy.

Bogost, Ian. "MOOCs Are Marketing: The Question Is, Can They Be More?" *Blog: Ian Bogost* (July 18, 2012). http://bogost.com/writing/blog/moocs_are _marketing/.

Brand, Stewart. *The Media Lab: Inventing the Future at MIT.* New York: Viking, 1987.

Brooks, David. "The Campus Tsunami." *New York Times* (May 4, 2012).

Buchmann, Claudia, Vincent Roscigno, and Dennis Condron. "The Myth of Meritocracy? SAT Preparation, College Enrollment, Class, and Race in the United States." Paper Presented at the Annual Meeting of the American Sociological Association (August 10, 2006). http://citation.allacademic.com /meta/p104558_index.html.

Carey, Kevin. *The End of College: Creating the Future of Learning and the University of Everywhere.* New York: Riverhead Books, 2015.

"CCCC Position Statement: Principles for the Postsecondary Teaching of Writing." Conference on College Composition and Communication (2015). http://www .ncte.org/cccc/resources/positions/postsecondarywriting.

Chambliss, Daniel, and Christopher Takacs. *How College Works.* Cambridge: Harvard University Press, 2014.

Christensen, Clayton M. "Disruptive Innovation." *Key Concepts.* http://www .claytonchristensen.com/key-concepts/.

———. *The Innovator's Dilemma: When New Technologies Cause Great Firms to Fail.* Brighton: Harvard Business School Press, 1997.

Christensen, Clayton M., and Henry J. Eyring. *The Innovative University: Changing the DNA of Higher Education from the Inside Out.* San Francisco: Jossey-Bass, 2011.

Christensen, Gayle, Andrew Steinmetz, Brandon Alcorn, Amy Bennett, Deirdre Woods, and Ezekiel J. Emanuel. "The MOOC Phenomenon: Who Takes Massive Open Online Courses and Why? (working paper). http://poseidon01.ssrn. com/delivery.php?ID=693102115122094126013001112098012124025033010045057018088111122064105127106067113014024027057111007030003308

5065086007013119028011048088035048126120003024115127120119027069071
0650310830720711081201190061170060961270210900980990120050860 20123
003099066117&EXT=pdf.

"Colleges That Lead to Graduate School." *US News & World Report* (June 2, 2015). http://www.usnews.com/education/best-colleges/the-short-list-college /articles/2015/06/02/10-colleges-that-lead-to-graduate-school.

DeMillo, Richard A. *Abelard to Apple: The Fate of American Colleges and Universities*. Cambridge: The MIT Press, 2011.

"Did Peter Drucker actually say 'culture eats strategy for breakfast'—and if so, where/when?" *Quora*. https://www.quora.com/Did-Peter-Drucker-actually-say -culture-eats-strategy-for-breakfast-and-if-so-where-when.

"eCore: Georgia's College Core-Curriculum . . . Online." *University System of Georgia Website*. https://ecore.usg.edu.

Excelsior Online Writing Lab, http://owl.excelsior.edu.

Feynman, Richard, Robert B. Leighton, and Matthew Sands. *The Feynman Lectures on Physics: The New Millennium Edition*. New York: Basic Books, 2011.

"The Flame Challenge." *The Alan Alda Center for Communicating Science*. http:// www.centerforcommunicatingscience.org/flame-challenge-2015/.

Folsom, Ed, and Kenneth M. Price, eds. *The Walt Whitman Archive*. http://www .whitmanarchive.org.

Ford, Henry. *My Life and Work*. Garden City, NY: Doubleday, Page & Company, 1922.

Freeman, Scott, Sarah L. Eddy, Miles McDonough, Michelle K. Smith, Nnadozie Okoroafor, Hannah Jordt, and Mary Pat Wenderoth. "Active Learning Increases Student Performance in Science, Engineering, and Mathematics." *Proceedings of the National Academy of Sciences of the United States of America* 11, no. 23 (2014). http://www.pnas.org/content/111/23/8410.

Friedman, Thomas. "Come the Revolution." *New York Times* (May 16, 2012).

———. "The Professors' Big Stage." *New York Times* (March 6, 2013).

———. "Revolution Hits the Universities." *New York Times* (January 27, 2013). http://www.nytimes.com/2013/01/27/opinion/sunday/friedman-revolution -hits-the-universities.html.

Gardner, Lee, and Jeffrey R. Young. "California's Move Toward MOOCs Sends Shock Waves, but Key Questions Remain Unanswered." *Chronicle of Higher Education* (March 14, 2013). http://chronicle.com/article/A-Bold-Move -Toward-MOOCs-Sends/137903/.

Gladwell, Malcolm. "@Gladwell." Twitter (June 3, 2015).

Head, Karen J. "Are MOOCs the Future of General Education?" *Journal of General Education: A Curricular Commons of the Humanities and Sciences* 63, no. 4 (2014): 244–55.

———. "Here a MOOC, There a MOOC: But Will It Work for Freshman Composition." *Chronicle of Higher Education: The Wired Campus* (blog). January 24, 2013. http://chronicle.com/blogs/wiredcampus/here-a-mooc-there -a-mooc-but-will-it-work-for-freshman-composition/41883.

———. "The Hidden Costs of MOOCs." In *Invasion of the MOOCs,* edited by Steven Krause and Charlie Lowe, 53. Anderson: Parlor Press, 2014.

———. "Inside a MOOC in Progress." *Chronicle of Higher Education: The Wired Campus* (blog). June 21, 2013. http://chronicle.com/blogs/wiredcampus/inside -a-mooc-in-progress/44397.

———. "Left Off." *Inside Higher Ed* (June 25, 2015). https://www.insidehighered. com/advice/2014/06/25/essay-academics-who-are-advised-leave-their-associate -degrees-their-cvs.

———. "Lessons Learned from a Freshman Composition MOOC." *Chronicle of Higher Education: The Wired Campus* (blog). September 6, 2013. http:// chronicle.com/blogs/wiredcampus/lessons-learned-from-a-freshman- composition-mooc/46337.

———. "Massive Open Online Adventure: Teaching a MOOC is Not for the Faint-hearted (or the Untenured)." *Chronicle of Higher Education* (April 29, 2013). http://chronicle.com/article/Massive-Open-Online-Adventure/138803/.

———. "Of MOOCs and Mousetraps." *Chronicle of Higher Education: The Wired Campus* (blog). February 21, 2013. http://chronicle.com/blogs/wiredcampus/of -moocs-and-mousetraps/42487.

———. "The Single Canon: MOOCs and Academic Colonization." In *MOOCs and Open Education Around the World*, edited by Curtis J. Bonk, Mimi Miyoung Lee, and Thomas C. Reeves, 12–20. New York: Routledge, 2015.

———. "Sweating the Details of a MOOC in Progress." *Chronicle of Higher Education: The Wired Campus* (blog). April 3, 2013. http://chronicle.com /blogs/wiredcampus/sweating-the-details-of-a-mooc-in-progress/43315.

Herrington, TyAnna K. "Who Owns My Work? The State of Work for Hire in Academics in Technical Communication." *Journal of Business and Technical Communication* 13, no. 2 (1999): 125–153.

Hoffman, Reid, and Ben Casnocha. *The Start-up of You: Adapt to the Future, Invest Yourself, and Transform Your Career.* New York: Crown Business, 2012.

Jaschik, Scott. "Breakup in Florida." *Inside Higher Ed* (September 14, 2015). https://

www.insidehighered.com/news/2015/09/14/u-florida-renegotiating-contract
-pearson-provide-services-uf-online.

———. "MOOC Mess." *Inside Higher Ed* (February 4, 2013). https://www
.insidehighered.com/news/2013/02/04/coursera-forced-call-mooc-amid
-complaints-about-course.

———. "Out of a Job." *Inside Higher Ed* (August 6, 2014). https://www.
insidehighered.com/news/2014/08/06/u-illinois-apparently-revokes-job-offer
-controversial-scholar.

Kaplan, Sarah. "Malcolm Gladwell: 'If Billionaires Don't Step Up, Harvard Will
Soon Be Down to Its Last $30 Billion.'" *Washington Post* (June 5, 2015). http://
www.washingtonpost.com/news/morning-mix/wp/2015/06/05/malcolm
-gladwell-if-billionaires-dont-step-up-harvard-will-soon-be-down-to-its-last-30
-billion/.

King, Andrew A., and Baijir Baatartogtokh. "How Useful Is the Theory of
Disruptive Innovation?" *MIT Sloan Management Review* (September 15, 2015).
http://sloanreview.mit.edu/article/how-useful-is-the-theory-of-disruptive-
innovation/?utm_source=twitter&utm_medium=social&utm
_campaign=featsept15.

Kovalik, Daniel. "Death of an Adjunct." *Pittsburgh Post Gazette* (September 18,
2013). http://www.post-gazette.com/Op-Ed/2013/09/18/Death-of-an-adjunct
/stories/201309180224.

Lepore, Jill. "The Disruption Machine: What the Gospel of Innovation Gets
Wrong." *New Yorker* (June 23, 2014). http://www.newyorker.com
/magazine/2014/06/23/the-disruption-machine.

Lessig, Lawrence. *The Future of Ideas: The Fate of the Commons in a Connected
World.* New York: Random House, 2001.

Lewin, Tamar. "Master's Degree Is New Frontier of Study Online." *New York Times*
(August 18, 2013).

Lewis, Harry. *Excellence Without a Soul: How a Great University Forgot Education.*
New York: Public Affairs, 2006.

McElroy, Tom. "Jamshed Bharucha Resigning as President of Cooper Union."
Huffington Post (June 10, 2015). http://www.huffingtonpost.com/2015/06/10
/jamshed-bharucha-resigning_n_7558284.html.

"NCTE Position Statement on Machine Scoring." National Council of Teachers
of English (2013). http://www.ncte.org/positions/statements/machine
_scoring.

"Nontraditional Undergraduates/Definitions and Data." *US Department of*

Education Institute for Educational Sciences: National Center for Educational Statistics. https://nces.ed.gov/pubs/web/97578e.asp.

Obama, Barack. "Remarks by the President on Opportunity for All and Skills for America's Workers." *White House: Office of the Press Secretary.* https://www .whitehouse.gov/the-press-office/2014/01/30/remarks-president-opportunity -all-and-skills-americas-workers.

Occupational Outlook Handbook: Postsecondary Teachers. United States Department of Labor: Bureau of Labor Statistics (2015). http://www.bls.gov/ooh/education -training-and-library/postsecondary-teachers.htm.

Ollstein, Alice. "Why Marco Rubio Owes Philosophy Majors an Apology." *Think Progress* (November 10, 2015). http://thinkprogress.org/ politics/2015/11/10/3721387/why-marco-rubio-owes-philosophy-majors-an -apology/.

Pappano, Laura. "The Year of the MOOC." *New York Times* (November 4, 2012).

Parry, Marc, Kelly Field, and Beckie Supiano. "The Gates Effect." *Chronicle of Higher Education* (July 14, 2013). http://chronicle.com/article/The-Gates-Effect/140323?cid=trend_right_wc.

Perelman, Les. "Construct Validity, Length, Score, and Time in Holistically Graded Writing Assessments: The Case against Automated Essay Scoring (AES)." In *International Advances in Writing Research: Cultures, Places, Measures,* edited by Charles Bazerman, Chris Dean, Jessica Early, Karen Lunsford, Suzie Null, Paul Rogers, and Amanda Stansell. 121–50. Anderson: Parlor Press, 2012.

Purdue Online Writing Lab. https://owl.english.purdue.edu/owl/.

Reeves, Thomas C. "How Do You Know They Are Learning? The Importance of Alignment in Higher Education." *International Journal of Learning Technology* 2, no. 4 (2006): 294–309.

"Response to Friedman." *Term Paper Warehouse.* http://www.termpaperwarehouse. com/essay-on/Response-To-Friedman/283337.

Rice, Andrew. "Anatomy of a Campus Coup." *New York Times Magazine* (September 16, 2012). http://www.nytimes.com/2012/09/16/magazine/teresa-sullivan-uva-ouster.html.

Rivard, Ry. "Humans Fight Over Robo-Readers." *Inside Higher Ed* (March 15, 2013). https://www.insidehighered.com/news/2013/03/15/professors-odds-machine-graded-essays.

Rodriguez, Osvaldo. "The Concept of Openness Behind c- and x-MOOCs (Massive Open Online Courses)." *Open Praxis* 5, no. 1 (2013): 67–73. http:// openpraxis.org/index.php/OpenPraxis/article/viewFile/42/12.

Rolstad, Kelly, and Kathleen Kesson. "Unschooling, Then and Now."
Journal of Unschooling and Alternative Learning 7, no. 14 (2013): 28-71.
http://jual.nipissingu.ca/wp-content/uploads/sites/25/2014/06/v72142
.pdf.

Sandel, Michael. *Justice: What's the Right Thing to Do?* New York: Farrar, Straus &
Giroux, 2010.

Schon, Donald A. *The Reflective Practitioner: How Professionals Think in Action.*
New York: Basic Books, 1983.

Schweers, Jeff. "Firm Will Get about $186 Million to Manage UF Online."
Gainesville Sun (March 27, 2014). http://www.gainesville.com/article
/20140327/articles/140329618.

Scientific American Frontiers. Public Broadcasting Service. http://www.pbs.org/saf
/alan.htm.

Shapiro, Judith. "The Digital Natives Are Restless." *Inside Higher Ed* (August 21,
2014). https://www.insidehighered.com/views/2014/08/21/essay-technology
-issues-facing-students-and-faculty-members.

Shirky, Clay. "Why I Just Asked My Students to Put Their Laptops Away." *Clay
Shirky* (blog). September 8, 2014. https://medium.com/@cshirky/why-i-just
-asked-my-students-to-put-their-laptops-away-7f5f7c50f368.

Spellings, Margaret. "A Test of Leadership: Charting the Future of US Higher
Education." *US Department of Education website.* http://www2.ed.gov/about
/bdscomm/list/hiedfuture/reports/final-report.pdf.

Spiegel, Eric. "MOOCs Will Change the University Business Model: The
Opportunities—and Risks—in the MOOC Business Model." *Wall Street
Journal* (October 15, 2013). http://www.wsj.com/articles/SB1000142405270230
456100457913536326607297.

Stratford, Michael. "Corinthian Closes for Good." *Inside Higher Ed* (April 27,
2015). https://www.insidehighered.com/news/2015/04/27/corinthian-ends-
operations-remaining-campuses-affecting-16000-students.

Straumsheim, Carl. "Place Your Bets." *Inside Higher Ed* (August 22, 2014).
https://www.insidehighered.com/news/2014/08/22/unsettled-ed-tech-market
-investments-are-easily-found.

Strauss, Valerie. "Trump University: Why the NY Attorney General Called It a
Scam." *Washington Post* (August 8, 2015). https://www.washingtonpost.com/
blogs/answer-sheet/wp/2015/08/08/trump-university-why-the-n-y-attorney
-general-called-it-a-scam/.

"Study: Who Teaches MOOCs?" *Inside Higher Ed* (October 26, 2015). https://

www.insidehighered.com/quicktakes/2015/10/26/study-who-teaches-moocs#.
Vi4Yvx3RwqQ.mailto.

"The University of Cambridge: The Age of Reforms (1800–82)." *British History
Online.* http://www.british-history.ac.uk/vch/cambs/vo13/pp235–265.

Toyama, Kentaro. *Geek Heresy: Rescuing Social Change from the Cult of Technology.*
New York: Public Affairs, 2015.

"University College London." *Wikipedia.* https://en.wikipedia.org/wiki/University
_College_London.

Wai, Jonathan, and Jenna Goudreau. "The 105 Smartest Public Colleges in
America." *Business Insider* (September 30, 2015). http://www.businessinsider
.com/the-105-smartest-public-colleges-in-america-2015–9.

Waters, John K. "Taking Competency-Based Credentials Seriously in
the Workforce." *Campus Technology Website* (May 11, 2016). https://
campustechnology.com/articles/2016/05/11/taking-competency-based-
credentials-seriously-in-the-workforce.aspx.

Watkins, Matthew. "Free Freshman Year? Texas State Hopes to Try It Out." *Texas
Tribune* (September 10, 2015). https://www.texastribune.org/2015/09/10/free
-freshman-year-texas-state-will-try-it-out/.

Western Governors University Website. http://www.wgu.edu.

Zickuhr, Kathryn, and Aaron Smith. "Home Broadband 2013." *Pew Research Center*
(2013). http://www.pewinternet.org/2013/08/26/home-broadband-2013.

Zimbardo, Philip G. *The Stanford Prison Experiment Website.* http://www
.prisonexp.org.

Index

competition, valorization of, 65–68

Composition 2.0, 21–26; access to and ownership of course materials, 65; assessment of program, 60, 64; assessment of students, 91–94, 95–96, 98; certification proposal, 56, 75–77; clothing and appearance of instructor, forum discussion about, 83, 110–14, 137; costs, 23, 39, 57; Coursera and, 22–23, 30, 47–49, 63–65, 74; diversity issues, 82–84; humanitarian benefits and, 137; inception of, 3–4; interactivity, 86; outside constituencies, dealing with, 63–64; platform issues, 92–94; priorities of MOOC technicians versus teachers and schools, 45–49; as research opportunity, 8, 56; as "series of disruptions," 35–36

composition courses: defined, 26–27; educational experience of author as composition teacher, 26–28; freshman composition MOOC taught by author (*see* Composition 2.0); machine-grading issues, 98–102; OWLs (Online Writing Labs), 9, 22; process skills, difficulties with assessing, 94–96; writing centers, 9, 11, 152

Conference on College Composition and Communication (CCCC), 95

consumer viewpoint of students, 77–79

contingent (nontenured or adjunct) faculty, 1, 54–55, 118–23, 135, 138

continuing education units (CEUs), 75

Cooper Union, 135

Copyright Act, professor exception, 64–65

Corinthian Colleges, 35

costs: efficiency arguments, 58–60; of higher education tuition, 6, 36, 38; monetization of free services, 74–75, 161; of MOOCs, 38–41, 56–58; of online education, 54–56; quality and, 86–87

Coursera: assessment process and, 63–65; certification program, 40, 56, 75–76; Composition 2.0 and, 22–23, 30, 47–49, 63–65, 74; composition courses, appropriateness for, 99; fashionable tutorials offered by, 11; Internet access issues, 92–93; MOOC phenomenon and, 5–6, 31; peer review and, 98; specialization tracks, 161; video and course design specific to, 39

Create-X innovation ecosystem, Georgia Tech, 156

Croce, Jim, "Bad, Bad Leroy Brown," 50

crowdsourcing, 134

"culture eats strategy for breakfast," 158

Darrow, Benjamin, 149

Davis, Houston, 26

Dead Poets' Society (film), 107, 108, 109

DeMillo, Richard: *Abelard to Apple: The Fate of American Colleges and Universities* (2011), 12, 15–19, 31, 43, 50–51, 122; business theory applied to higher education by, 53, 54, 58, 67; disruption innovation and, 31–33, 36–38, 43–44; on employability and education, 71, 80; Georgia Tech and, 2, 17–18, 123–24, 155; on hierarchical classification of schools, 126, 130–31;

as instructor, 50–51, 123–24, 125; on instructors, 104–5; on quasi-religious aspects of universities, 140–43

democratization, MOOCs as agents of, 126, 133

Desire to Learn, 159

digital humanities, 33

disabled students and instructors, 64, 113, 136–37

disadvantaged and poor students, 84, 85, 132, 136–37

discourse. *See* rhetoric

disruptive innovation, 29–51; business theory applied to higher education in, 29–32, 37–38; costs of MOOCs and, 38–41; defined, 5, 29–30; educational future of, 161–62; familiar situations, attempts to explain MOOCs in relation to, 35–36; global higher education economy, appeals to, 34–35; hierarchical classification of schools and, 126; history of change in universities and, 43–45; Internet and other technology comparisons, 36–38; ivory tower, technology-backward notion of universities and, 32–34, 38, 43–45; personal attention, student need for, 41–43; priorities of MOOC technicians versus teachers and schools, 45–49; rhetorical force of, 8, 30–33; teaching qualifications of main backers of, 50–51, 123–25

distance learning programs, 10–11

diversity issues, 80–84

Drucker, Peter, 158

Duke University, 96

Duquesne University, 121

e-Core, 63

ecosystem, education system viewed as, 30, 41, 53, 62–64, 153, 155–58

Edison, Thomas, 149

ed-tech entrepreneurs, 49, 50–51, 123–25

educational experience of author, 20–28; as composition teacher, 26–28; freshman composition MOOC taught by author (*See* Composition 2.0); as graduate student teaching assistant, 119–20; hierarchical classification of schools and, 126; personal educational background, 20–21, 72–73, 87

EdX, 5, 6, 11, 31, 55, 56, 106, 127

efficiency and quality issues, 58–60

elective system, 66, 71–72

Eliot, Charles, 66, 71

elite schools. *See* hierarchical classification of schools

email address, privacy and security concerns regarding, 114–15

employability and education, 69–89; access to online services, 84–86; certificates and certification, 74–77; consumer viewpoint of students, 77–79; degree and profession, conflation of, 69–70; diversity issues, 80–84; general foundational education, value of, 71–74; hierarchical classification of schools and, 128–32; job training, expecting universities to supply, 69–73; student-faculty interaction, 86–89; types of students attracted by online programs, 80–82

enabling technology curves, 37

English fluency issues, 82–83

entrepreneurial model for universities, 37

entrepreneurial opportunities for students, 156–57

entrepreneurs: in "ed tech," 49, 50–51, 123–25; with philosophy degrees, 70

Essa, Irfan, 2

ethos-promoting devices, 13–15

evaluation. *See* assessment and value determination

Excelsior College, 9, 49

Eyring, Henry: on adjunct instructors, 118, 120–23; business theory applied to higher education by, 46, 54–55, 66; on disruption innovation, 33, 38, 42, 46; expertise of, 123, 125; on hierarchical classification of schools, 126, 127–29; on humanitarian benefits of MOOCs, 140; *The Innovative University: Changing the DNA of Higher Education from the Inside Out* (2011), with Clayton Christensen, 12, 13–15, 45, 52, 122–23, 127; on values-based education, 143–45

Facebook, 134

faculty. *See* instructors

familiar situations, attempts to explain MOOCs in relation to, 35–36

Farmer Says, 102

Feynman, Richard, 104

films about teaching, 107–9

Fiorina, Carly, 18, 70

first-year writing MOOC taught by author. *See* Composition 2.0

Foley, James, 124

Folson, Ed, 33

Forbes, 70

Ford, Henry, 42

fragmentation of learning, 96–98

freshman composition MOOC taught by author. *See* Composition 2.0

Freshman Year for Free (Texas State University System), 55, 56

Friedman, Thomas, 5–6, 17, 32, 78, 136

Galil, Zvi, 99

Galileo, 130–31

Gandhi, Mohandas K., 82

Gates Foundation, 3, 8, 21–22, 24–25, 27, 39, 63–64, 96

General Motors, 32

Georgia, University System of, 26, 63, 96

Georgia Institute of Technology (Georgia Tech): apprenticeship model at, 128; author's freshman composition MOOC for (*see* Composition 2.0); Brittain Postdoctoral Teaching Fellowship Program, 1, 120; *Business Insider* ranking, 67; C21U (Center for 21st Century Universities), 2, 22–23, 24, 25, 57, 93, 154, 155; Create-X innovation ecosystem, 156; CULC (commons building), 156; DeMillo and, 2, 17–18, 123–24, 155; diversity at, 80–82, 83; educational background of author and, 20; elective system at, 71; "Grand Challenges" program, 156; hierarchical classification of schools and, 126–27; InVenture

Prize, 156; OMS (online master's program in computer science), students attracted by, 80–82, 161; online education at, 6, 10; Oxford Study Abroad Program, 15, 26, 116; Presidential Scholars Program, 68; public meetings on technological innovations, 1–3, 99, 148, 153–57; reaccreditation, 59; return on investment for education at, 79; Student Integrity Committee, 79; teaching loads at, 123–24; Vertically Integrated Projects program, 156; women students at, 81; writing center at, 9

humanities, arts, and social sciences, 69–70, 97

illocutionary force, 31
Indiana University, 10
individual attention, student need for, 38, 41–43, 58, 61–62, 86–89, 151–53
Inside Higher Ed, 35
Institutional Review Board (IRB), 59
instructors, 103–25; adoption of MOOCs affecting status of, 106; clothing and appearance of, in MOOC productions, 83, 109–14, 137; disruptive innovation, teaching qualifications of main backers of, 50–51, 123–25; films about teaching, 107–9; innovative pedagogy and, 157–60; as MOOC students, 84; nontenured (adjunct or contingent) faculty, 1, 54–55, 118–23, 135, 138; ownership of course materials, 64–65, 106; parental role of, 145; performance, teaching as, 103, 112; presenters apart from, 103–4; privacy and security concerns, 76–77, 114–17; as public face of institution, department, or discipline, 117–18; student-faculty relationship and interaction, 38, 41–43, 58, 61–62, 86–89, 151–53; "superstar professors," 104–7; teacher-centered approach of MOOCs, 103; teaching assistants, 41, 48, 51, 56, 57, 78, 95, 101, 106, 118–23; teaching loads, 123–25; tenured and tenure-track faculty, 3, 54–55, 77, 118, 120–21, 124, 127, 135, 144–45, 157

interactivity issues, 38, 41–43, 58, 61–62, 86–89, 151–53
international students, 80–81
Internet, introduction of MOOCs compared to, 36–38
Internet access, 84–86, 92
Internet bubble, 36, 74
InVenture Prize, Georgia Tech, 156
ivory tower, technology-backward notion of universities, 20, 32–34, 38, 43–45, 140–43

Jesuits, 43, 44
job training, expecting universities to supply, 69–73
Jobs, Steve, 162

Kaczynski, Theodore (Unabomber), 46
Kaplan, Sarah, 132
Kim, Joshua M., 49
King, Martin Luther, Jr., 82, 83
Kodak, 29
Koller, Daphne, 49, 62–63, 88, 99, 136
Kovalik, Daniel, 121

LDS Business College, 139
LDS Church (Church of Jesus Christ of Latter-day Saints, or Mormons), 14, 122, 138–40
Leahy, Bill, 77
learning management systems (LMSs), 159–60
Lessig, Lawrence, 37
Lewis, Harry, 52–53
liberal arts education, 69–73, 97
literacy, technological, 85–86

signature, privacy and security concerns regarding, 76–77

Signature Track (Coursera certification program), 75–76

Silicon Valley, 34, 83–84, 92

Sinclair, Upton, 149

Slow Food Movement, 61

Smith, Adam, 66

social sciences, arts, and humanities, 69–70, 97

Socrates and Socratic method, 19, 105

soft skills, 69

Southern Association of Colleges and Schools, 59

Southern New Hampshire University, 133

Spelling, Margaret, and Spelling Commission Report, 52

Spiegel, Eric, 34

standardized testing, 90–94, 96–97

Stanford Prison Experiment, 59

Stanford University, 5, 6, 45, 49, 58, 70, 143

State Higher Education Executive Officer Association, 26, 157

STEAM education, 70

STEM education, 19, 70, 73, 94–95, 98, 102

St. Mary's College of Maryland, 129

student-faculty relationship and interaction, 38, 41–43, 58, 61–62, 86–89, 151–53

students: disabled, 64, 136–37; entrepreneurial opportunities for, 156–57; graduate student teaching assistants, 41, 48, 51, 56, 57, 78, 95, 101, 106, 118–23; individual attention and interactivity, need for, 38, 41–43, 58, 61–62, 86–89, 151–53; instructors as MOOC students, 84; international, 80–81; nontraditional, 21, 56, 72, 108; plagiarism by, 78–79; poor and disadvantaged, 84, 85, 132, 136–37; types attracted by online programs, 80–82; women, 81, 83. *See also* assessment and value determination: consumer viewpoint of students, 77–79

Studio 54, 134

Sullivan, Theresa, 6

SUNY-Plattsburgh, 129

Takacs, Christopher, 42, 117–18

teachers. *See* instructors

teaching assistants, 41, 48, 51, 56, 57, 78, 95, 101, 106, 118–23

Technische Universität Dortmund, 106

technological literacy, 85–86

technology, utopian views of, 148–62; future of MOOCs and, 160–62; Georgia Tech public meeting on technological innovation and, 148, 153–57; historical background, 149; instructors and innovative pedagogy, 157–60; interactivity issues, 38, 41–43, 58, 61–62, 86–89, 151–53; laptops and other devices in traditional classrooms, pros and cons of, 150–51; LMSs (learning management systems), 159–60; Toyama's *Geek Heresy* and, 148–50, 152, 153, 155, 159–60

technology-backward, ivory tower notion of universities, 20, 32–34, 38, 43–45, 140–43 television networks, 36–37

Tennessee Technology Center (TTC), 129, 131, 133

tenured and tenure-track faculty, 3, 54–55, 77, 118, 120–21, 124, 127, 135, 144–45, 157

Texas State University System, 7, 55, 56

Texas Tribune, 7

Thomas Aquinas, 105

Thrun, Sebastian, 49, 99

tithing at BYU-Idaho, 122, 140

To Sir, with Love (film), 107, 109

Toyama, Kentaro, *Geek Heresy: Rescuing Social Change from the Cult of Technology* (2015), 148–50, 152, 153, 155, 159–60

Toyota, 32

Trump "University," 60

tuition costs, 6, 36, 38

tutoring or coaching, 152–53

Twitter, 132, 144

Udacity, 5, 6, 11, 31, 49, 80, 99

UF Online, 55, 56

Unabomber (Theodore Kaczynski), 46

Universitat Politècnica de Catalunya (UPC), Barcelona, 142–43

University of Berlin, 66

University of California–Berkeley, 46, 150

University of Florida, 55, 56

University of Georgia, 10

University of Illinois Urbana-Champaign, 144

University of London, 44

University of Nebraska, 33, 130

University of Padua, Italy, 32, 130

University of Paris, 43

University of Pennsylvania, 84

University of Phoenix, 81–82

University System of Georgia, 26, 63, 96

University of Tennessee at Knoxville, 130

University of Virginia, 6

US News and World Report, 91, 128, 129

utopian views of technology. *See* technology, utopian views of

value determination. *See* assessment and value determination

Vertically Integrated Projects program, Georgia Tech, 156

Vojtko, Margaret Mary, 121, 125

Wayne State University, 129

Western Governors University, 55

Whitman Digital Archive, 33

Wikipedia, 37

Williams, Robin, 108

Wirth, Fatima, 2

women in educational system, 81, 83, 109–14

writing centers, 9, 11, 152

writing courses. *See* composition courses

x-MOOCs, 49

Year of the MOOC (2012), 5, 31

YouTube, 36

Zimbardo, Philip G., 59